"church bulletin bits" #2

"church bulletin bits"

volume #2

GEORGE W. KNIGHT
COMPILER

BAKER BOOK HOUSE
Grand Rapids, Michigan 49506

Copyright 1980 by
Baker Book House Company

ISBN: 0-8010-5424-9

Fourth printing, February 1984

Contents

Preface

Churches must have a mammoth appetite for short fillers on many different subjects! How else do you explain the popularity of my first compilation of *Church Bulletin Bits, volume 1*, published five years ago? Thousands of churches bought the book, published the fillers in their newsletters and bulletins—and now they're asking for more. I'm delighted to respond to this need with *Church Bulletin Bits, volume 2*. It's a compilation of totally new and different items, guaranteed to fill out your church publications with pep and enthusiasm.

Several of the subject headings that appeared in the original book are repeated in this volume. But many new subject areas have been added to help you fill your church publications with more interesting material on a broader range of topics.

When you publish one of these fillers in your church newsletter or bulletin, don't forget to write it down in the "Record of Publication" section at the back of the book. This will give you a valuable record to keep you from reprinting the same items in the same places over and over again.

These fillers don't carry a line that reads, "Reprint at will," but that's exactly what this book encourages you to do. I hope you find *Church Bulletin Bits, volume 2* as handy and practical as the first compilation of these gems of wisdom.

GEORGE W. KNIGHT

1
Living the Christian Life

1. A CHRISTIAN'S ABC'S

Attend church faithfully.

Be careful what you say.

Consider carefully every decision.

Do right; fear to do wrong.

Endure hardships without complaint.

Forsake not your family and friends.

Go no place that would harm your influence.

Hate no one; do good to every person.

Ignore no person; practice hospitality.

Join hands with other righteous people.

Keep your mind pure.

Lie not; always tell the truth.

Minister to the needy.

Never try to appear to be what you are not.

Oppose evil.

Pay your debts promptly.

Question not the motives of others.

Remember all of God's gifts.

Sacrifice money rather than principle.

Think before you speak.

Use your time wisely.

Value the Bible above all books.

Watch your temper.

X-ray your thoughts.

Yield not to temptation.

Zealously labor for the Lord.

2. MOST IMPORTANT WORDS

6/9/85 The six most important words: "I admit I made a mistake."

The five most important words: "You did a good job."

The four most important words: "What is your opinion?"

The three most important words: "If you please."

The two most important words: "Thank you."

The one most important word: "We."

The least important word: "I."

3. THE DISEASE OF CRITICISM

The church is made up of imperfect people. All of us have our faults. The amazing thing is that God has been able to work through imperfect Christians. He has never had a chance with any other kind.

The Christian who becomes infected with criticism of others loses sight of the major cause. He gets engrossed in details and misses the supreme design. His eyes wander from the crucified

Christ to focus on the faults of those for whom Christ died. This causes his spiritual life to dry up.

Wanted: Christians who overlook the faults of others as easily as they do their own.

4. THE "IZE" HAVE IT

Here are seven simple ways to begin living a more abundant, productive, and rewarding life:

Memorize at least one great truth every day. It may be an inspiring poem, an especially helpful verse of Scripture, or a favorite quotation. What you memorize becomes a part of your life, your character, and your future.

Crystallize your goals, your aspirations, and your ambitions. Write them down and include a workable timetable for their accomplishment.

Specialize in some particular skill. Become an expert and an authority and you will never lack for a job.

Neutralize your fears, your doubts, and your anxieties through the power of prayer, meditation, and a positive mental attitude.

Minimize your shortcomings, your liabilities, and your deficiencies. Because you were designed by a Master Architect, you are greater than you think!

Maximize your abilities, your talents, your potential, and your possibilities. Accentuate your positives.

Recognize the good in others, the beauty of friendship, the splendor of love, and the joy of service. Train your eyes to look for the best in others, and others will see the best in you.

— William Arthur Ward

5. IN GRAVE DANGER

Anyone who professes to be a Christian is in grave danger:

When he rejects the clear statements of the Bible because "they don't speak to me."

When he substitutes the opinions of human beings for the revelation of God as found in the Scriptures.

When he thinks he can receive Christ but reject what the Bible teaches about his person and work.

When he thinks it possible to have Christianity without Christian doctrine—the content on which the Christian faith is built.

When he substitutes activity in the church and its programs for personal spiritual nurture.

When he gets so busy with the affairs of the world that regular prayer and Bible study are pushed aside by his heavy schedule.

6. SEVEN MINDS

1. Mind your tongue. Don't let it speak hasty, cruel, unkind, or wicked words.

2. Mind your eyes. Don't permit them to look at degrading books, pictures, or objects.

3. Mind your ears. Don't let them listen to evil songs or words.

4. Mind your lips. Don't let strong drink enter your mouth.

5. Mind your hands. Don't let them do evil to others.

6. Mind your feet. Don't let them follow in the footsteps of evil.

7. Mind your heart. Don't let the love of sin dwell in it. Ask Jesus Christ to make it his throne.

7. I DARE YOU

I dare you to spend more time reading God's Word than the daily newspaper.

I dare you to face your doubts and conquer them.

I dare you to brave the snickers of your friends and live in the simple style which will enable you to spend more time with Christ.

I dare you to challenge your friends to live up to their professed religion.

I dare you to take Christ with you into the classroom, office, and workshop.

I dare you to tell the truth in love whenever you speak.

I dare you to live above the average standard of morals and be really virtuous.

I dare you to be honest with yourself and evaluate the way you spend your leisure time in the light of your love for Christ.

I dare you to be courageous and willing to accept criticism by trying to start some new form of Christian ministry.

I dare you to throw your whole soul into the worship of God every time you meet for that purpose.

I dare you to work half as hard to win people to Christ as you work for your business.

I dare you to act as if you believe that Jesus is the Christ.

—Norvel Young

8. LOOKING ON THE OUTSIDE

Most of us judge people by looking at certain external characteristics. Check up on yourself. Mark each of the following "true" or "false."

1. A person who doesn't look you in the eye is likely to be dishonest.

2. A receding chin indicates lack of will power.

3. Blondes are apt to be less trustworthy than brunettes.

4. Fat people are typically good-natured.

5. Ears pointed at the top warn of foxiness, selfishness, or even dishonesty.

6. Wrinkles at the outer corners of the eyes show that a person has a sense of humor.

7. Curly hair is a symptom of exuberance and vitality.

8. A high, bulging forehead is a sign of superior brain power.

9. Cold hands are a sign of affectionate disposition.

Psychologists who use these questions to test personnel administrators say a score of seven correct answers means you're probably a pretty good judge of character. A score of six is passing. A score below five indicates you judge people on the basis of false stereotypes.

And what are the correct answers? According to scientists who have checked these beliefs against actual fact, all are false.

9. A GARDEN

If you are making a garden
  Where flowers or vegetables grow,
You must work the ground and plant the seed
  Carefully, row on row.

A garden is a great deal of work,
  Back-breaking and tiring toil,
But you're working with God and his miracles
  When you're working with the soil.

And that's the way with little ones
  Entrusted to your care,
We must work the ground and plant the seeds
  And tend them with a prayer.

Plant seeds of trust and faith and hope,
  And they will grow big and strong;
Pull out all hate and envy and greed,
  For these are the weeds of wrong.

This truth we know about a child—
  We cannot train him alone,
But we and God find a miracle
  When the child to a man has grown.

                                        —Author unknown

10. WHO IS HE KIDDING?

When a person claims he can't stay awake through a twenty-minute sermon but he stays home with his 700-column newspaper, who is he kidding?

When a man says Sunday is his only day of rest but he gets up at 4:30 to go fishing or spends the day on a golf course, who is he kidding?

When a person says the church pews are too hard but he sits on a bleacher for hours and watches football players push one another back and forth across a mud lot, who is he kidding?

When a person says he can't afford to tithe but he lives in a comfortable home, drives a new car, and eats well, who is he kidding?

When a man says he doesn't have time for Christ and the church but he spends evenings shopping, bowling, watching television, and going to clubs, who is he kidding?

He's certainly not kidding God.

11. THE STERLING CHRISTIAN

1. One who moves his church membership when he moves to a new community.

2. One who gives regularly and cheerfully to the support of his church.

3. One who lives a life that is an asset and not a liability to the cause of Christ.

4. One who knows, believes in, and practices the doctrines and teachings of the Bible.

5. One who reads his Bible and prays sincerely to God each day.

6. One who seeks the salvation of his family, friends, neighbors, and all others who are lost.

7. One who recognizes that the church is bigger than him and his opinion.

8. One who seeks to improve his Christian life through reading good Christian literature.

9. One who is always ready to forgive others as Christ has forgiven him.

12. THE 23RD CHANNEL

The TV is my shepherd; my spiritual growth shall want. It maketh me to sit down and do nothing for his name's sake, because it requireth all my leisure time. It keepeth me from doing my duty as a Christian because it presenteth so many good shows that I must see.

It restoreth my knowledge of the things of the world, and keepeth me from the study of God's Word. It leadeth me in the paths of failing to attend church and doing nothing in the kingdom of God.

Yea, though I live to be a hundred, I shall keep viewing my TV as long as it will work, for it is my closest companion. Its sounds and pictures, they comfort me.

It presenteth entertainment before me and keepeth me from doing important things with my family. It fills my head with ideas which differ from those in the Word of God.

Surely, no good thing will come of my life because of so many wasted hours, and I shall dwell in my remorse and bitter memories forever.

2
New Year's
Messages

---

13. WHAT OF TOMORROW?

I do not know what still awaits,
Or what the morrow brings;
But with the glad salute of faith,
I hail its opening wings!

For this I know—that in my Lord
Shall all my needs be met;
And I can trust the heart of him
Who has not failed me yet.

— Author unknown

14. GOOD ADVICE FOR THE NEW YEAR

If you haven't made your New Year's resolutions yet, how about these from Paul's letter to the Romans?

Let us have no imitation Christian love. Let us have a genuine break with evil and a real devotion to good. Let us have real warm affection for one another as between brothers, and a willingness to let the other man have the credit.

Let us not allow slackness to spoil our work and let us keep the fires of the spirit burning, as we do our work for God.

Base your happiness on your hope in Christ. When trials come, endure them patiently: steadfastly maintain the habit of prayer.

Give freely to fellow Christians in want, never grudging a meal or a bed to those who need them. And as for those who try to make your life a misery, bless them. Don't curse, bless.

Share the happiness of those who are happy, and the sorrow of those who are sad. Live in harmony with one another. Don't become snobbish but take a real interest in ordinary people. Don't become set in your own opinions.

Don't pay back a bad turn by a bad turn, to *anyone*. Don't say, "It doesn't matter what people think," but see that your public behavior is above criticism.

As far as your responsibility goes, live at peace with everyone. Never take vengeance into your own hands, my dear friends: stand back and let God punish if he will. . . .

Don't allow yourself to be overpowered with evil. Take the offensive—overpower evil by good! (Romans 12, Phillips translation).

15. THE GOD WHO KNOWS

I do not know the future,
  But I know the God who knows,
And in his perfect wisdom,
  Unknowing, I repose.

What good could come of knowing?
  How little I could do
To meet the joys or sorrows
  That I am coming to!

I do not know the future,
  But I know the God who knows,
I make his love my study
  And follow where he goes.

The path, its joys and sorrows,
  I do not care to trace;

Content to know his goodness,
His mercy, and his grace.

—William Luff

16. PRAYER FOR THE NEW YEAR

God give you faith this coming year!
The faith that will not fail in keenest test;
That trusts and sings in midst of fire and storm,
And dares rely upon his Word and rest.

God give you hope this coming year!
The hope that through the darkness sees afar—
The purifying hope that fondly waits
The rising of the Bright and Morning Star.

God give you love this coming year!
His own great love that burns out for the lost;
That intercedes, and waits, and suffers long—
That never fails, nor stops to count the cost.

—Margaret D. Armstrong

17. HOW TO LIVE THE NEW YEAR 1/5/85

Life is a journey; I will live it trustingly: "though I walk through the valley of the shadow . . . I will fear no evil: for thou art with me" (Psalm 23:4).

Life is a task; I will live it obediently: "we keep his commandments, and do those things that are pleasing in his sight" (1 John 3:22).

Life is a mission; I will live it helpfully: "Be ye kind one to another, tenderhearted, forgiving one another" (Ephesians 4:32).

Life is a contest; I will live it earnestly: "Watch ye, stand fast in the faith, quit you like men, be strong" (1 Corinthians 16:13).

Life is a battle; I will live it courageously: "Be strong and of a good courage; be not afraid; for the Lord thy God is with thee" (Joshua 1:9).

18. THE UNKNOWN FUTURE

Life is a book in volumes three—
The past, the present, and the yet-to-be.
The past is written and laid away,
The present we're writing every day,
And the last and best of volumes three
Is locked from sight—God keeps the key.

—Author unknown

19. THE ROSE

It is only a tiny rosebud—
  A flower of God's design,
But I cannot unfold the petals
  With these clumsy hands of mine.

The secret of unfolding flowers
  Is not known to such as I—
The flower God opens so sweetly
  In my hands would fade and die.

If I cannot unfold a rosebud,
  This flower of God's design,
Then how can I think I have wisdom
  To unfold this life of mine?

So I'll trust him for his leading
  Each moment of every day,
And I'll look to him for guidance
  Each step of the pilgrim way.

For the pathway that lies before me
  My Heavenly Father knows—
I'll trust him to reveal the moments
  Just as he unfolds the rose.

—Author unknown

20

3
Church Attendance and Support

---

20. SOME SOBERING QUESTIONS

Would you like:

To live in a country where there are no churches?

To see all pastors, teachers, missionaries, and workers for righteousness go on strike?

To see all churches close their doors on Sunday?

To see the kingdom of God grind to a halt because churches ran out of money?

To see the blessings of God withdrawn from your country?

Then take stock:

Am I doing my part to keep events like these from happening?

Do I ride free on the sacrifices of others?

Does Christianity show in my daily life?

Does the Christian faith mean getting or giving to me?

21

21. I AM YOUR CHURCH

I am your church. I am here because you built me. I am beautifully situated in your midst. In the center of your neighborhood I will be a cherished landmark to the people who will come to my doors in the coming years. You built me, remember, because you know your life is incomplete without me.

I am your church. But I am not here simply to adorn. I am here to serve. Your children and growing youth come to me to be taught the ways of the Lord. Your brides and grooms come to my altar so their marriages will be sanctified by divine blessings.

I am your church. I comfort your sick and sorrowing. I bury your dead and offer rest to the weary. Pardon and peace are my messages to the sin-burdened soul. My message of mercy brings new life. To your aged I give courage and security. I cause their children to call them blessed.

I am your church. My doors are open to all — rich or poor, bond or free. My pulpit rings out the message of good will to men, of peace and pardon and a Saviour's love to all. I teach you the way of life and guide you on the road to heaven.

I am your church. Come and worship and support me, and I will serve you all your days.

22. NEEDED: FAITHFUL CHRISTIANS

If you had a car that failed to start every seventh day, you probably wouldn't call it faithful. If you had a watch that usually was accurate but failed once every ten days, you would take it to the repair shop. If your hot water heater greeted you with cold water on some morning, you wouldn't regard it as dependable.

Some Christians are as undependable at attending church as the items mentioned above. Remember the words of Jesus: "Be thou faithful unto death, and I will give thee a crown of life" (Revelation 2:10b).

23. DON'T JOIN THE PERFECT CHURCH

If you should find the perfect church

Without one fault or smear,
For goodness sake! Don't join that church—
You'd spoil the atmosphere.

If you should find the perfect church
Where all anxieties cease,
Then pass it by, lest joining it,
You mar the masterpiece.

If you should find the perfect church,
Then don't you ever dare
To tread upon such holy ground—
You'd be a misfit there.

But since no perfect church exists,
Made of imperfect men,
Then let's quit looking for that church
And love the church we're in.

Yes, let's keep working in our church
Until the resurrection,
And then we each will join that church
Without an imperfection!

—Author unknown

24. ESSENTIALS FOR A GREAT CHURCH

1. A regenerated church membership.

2. A praying membership.

3. A working membership.

4. A cooperating membership.

5. A membership with a vision and the faith to see that vision become reality.

6. A membership where everybody is somebody.

7. A membership where nobody tries to be number one but everybody is willing to work for the common good.

25. REAL SERVICE?

I'll go where you want me to go, dear Lord,

Real service is what I desire;
I'll say what you want me to say, dear Lord—
But don't ask me to sing in the choir.

I'll say what you want me to say, dear Lord,
I'd love to see things come to pass;
But don't ask me to teach girls and boys, dear Lord—
I'd rather just sit in my class.

I'll do what you want me to do, dear Lord,
I yearn for the kingdom to thrive;
I'll give you my nickles and dimes, dear Lord—
But please don't ask me to tithe.

I'll go where you want me to go, dear Lord,
I'll say what you want me to say;
But I'm busy just now with myself, dear Lord—
I'll help you some other day.

—Author unknown

26. I NEED MY CHURCH

I am a part of the church—one among many—but I am one.

I need the church for the development of my spiritual life. I can't be what I need to be without the church.

The church may be human in its organization, but it is divine in its purpose. That purpose is to point people toward God.

Participating in the privileges of the church, I shall also share in its responsibilities, taking it upon myself to carry my fair share of the load, not grudgingly, but joyfully.

If I fail in my responsibilities, the church fails; if I succeed, the church succeeds.

I shall not wait to be drafted for service in my church. I shall volunteer, saying, "Here am I, send me."

I shall be loyal in my attendance, generous in my gifts, kind in my criticism, creative in my suggestions, loving in my attitudes.

I shall give to my church my interest, enthusiasm, and devotion—most of all, myself.

27. SUNDAY ISN'T SUNDAY WITHOUT CHURCH

I know a thousand things to do when Sunday rolls
* around,*
But most of them will interfere with worship, I have
* found;*
If I use the day for pleasure, I have conscience in the
* lurch—*
For Sunday isn't Sunday unless I go to church.

A man may tinker with his car, or take his shotgun out,
Or he may grab a rod and reel and try to catch a trout;
A woman has her household tasks, like washing socks and
* shirts—*
But Sunday isn't Sunday to those neglecting church.

We can follow inclination and just loaf around all day,
We can eat and sleep and eat some more but take no time
* to pray;*
The habit of indifference will any soul besmirch—
For Sunday is never Sunday unless we go to church.

—Author unknown

28. HOW TO JUDGE A GREAT CHURCH

What does it take to make a great church?

Not soft seats and subdued light, but courageous leadership.

Not sweet tones of the organ, but sweet personalities.

Not tall towers, but lofty vision.

Not a big budget, but big hearts.

Not money received, but service rendered.

Not a large membership, but God's presence.

Not what it has done in the past, but what it is doing for Christ
now and in the future.

29. OR DO YOU JUST BELONG?

Are you an active member—
* The kind who would be missed—*

Or are you just contented
  That your name is on the list?

Do you attend the meetings
  And mingle with the flock?
Or do you stay at home
  And criticize and knock?

Do you take an active part
  To help the work along?
Or are you satisfied to be
  Of those that just belong?

Do you ever voluntarily
  Help at the guiding stick?
Or leave the work to just a few
  And talk about the clique?

Come out to meetings often
  And help with hands and heart;
Don't be just a member,
  But take an active part.

Think this over, member,
  You know right from wrong—
Are you an active member
  Or do you just belong?

—Author unknown

30. THE RIGHT SIDE

Every Sunday morning an old man walked several blocks to the church in his neighborhood. He was deaf, so he couldn't hear the sermon, the music of the choir, or the congregational singing.

"Why do you spend your Sundays in that church when you can't hear a word?" a neighbor asked.

"I want the people around here to know which side I'm on," he replied.

How about you? Do your neighbors know which side you're on, on Sunday morning?

31. TEN WAYS TO KILL A CHURCH

1. Don't come.

2. If you do come, always arrive late.

3. After every service let it be known loud and clear that you "didn't get anything out of the service."

4. Never accept a job or leadership position in the church. It's much better to stand on the sidelines and criticize.

5. Visit other churches about half of the time just to show your pastor and fellow church members that you aren't tied to them.

6. Make the paid leaders of the church earn their salaries. Make them do all the work and blame them if it isn't done.

7. Sit toward the back of the church and never sing or participate in the service in any way.

8. Never pay in advance. Wait to see if you are going to get your money's worth.

9. Never encourage the pastor.

10. Be sure to point out any faults of your church to any guests who might be present for the service. They might never notice these faults without your help.

32. SITTER, QUITTER, OR GETTER?

I'm a sitter. I just want to sit and enjoy the service and do nothing.

I'm a quitter. I taught a class once, but I've served my time. I even visited for the church a time or two, but no one was at home. If anything is done in this church, somebody else will have to do it.

I'm a getter. The more I think about God and his salvation, the more I want to do for him. Even today he is preparing a place for me in eternity. He hasn't stopped working for me, so I will continue to work for him.

33. THE INACTIVE CHURCH MEMBER'S CALENDAR

January—I hereby resolve to start attending church this year. But first I have to get over the holidays. They really take a lot out of you.

February—Weather's terrible. I'll start when it gets a bit warmer. My blood is just too thin this time of year.

March—Lots of sickness going around now. Guess I'd better stay away from all those bugs.

April—Easter . . . big crowds . . . they won't miss me.

May—I've been inside all winter. Now that the weather is better, it's time to go to the park.

June—I'll wait until the baby is older. How on earth do some people take their babies to church when they are just a few weeks old?

July—This heat is terrific! That air conditioning in the church probably isn't working right. Besides, we've got that cabin and boat for Sundays.

August—The pastor's on vacation. He'll never know I missed. Never liked those guest preachers, anyway. But when he gets back. . .

September—School's started. My vacation threw me behind in my work. It'll take me a little while to get back in the swing of things.

October—The leaves are beautiful this time of year. I can worship God outdoors just as well.

November — Getting colder . . . can't stand warm church buildings. All stuffy inside. I'll start back when it gets warmer.

December—Christmas! I just don't have time for church this month. I'll just resolve now to start going to church next year.

34. THINGS THAT BREAK YOUR HEART

To see little boys and girls at church without their parents.

To realize that some parents never experience the joy of sitting with their children in a worship service.

To know that one day — when their hearts are broken and their dreams are crushed — these parents will look back at these years as the time when seeds of disaster were sown in the lives of their children.

35. A MODERN VERSION OF NOAH'S ARK

And the Lord said unto Noah, "Where is the ark which I commanded you to build?"

And Noah said unto the Lord: "Verily, I have had three carpenters off sick. The gopher wood supplier hath let me down, yea, even though the gopher wood hath been on order for six months. What can I do, O Lord?"

And God said unto Noah, "I want that ark finished within seven days."

And Noah said, "It will be so."

But it was not so. And the Lord said unto Noah, "What seemeth to be the trouble this time?"

And Noah said unto the Lord: "Mine subcontractor hath gone bankrupt. The pitch which Thou commandest me to put on the outside and inside of the ark hath not arrived. The plumber and his crew hath gone on strike. Lord, I am undone."

And the Lord grew angry and said: "What about the animals, the male and the female of every sort that I ordered to come unto thee to keep their seed alive upon the face of the earth?"

And Noah said, "They have been delivered unto the wrong address, but they should arrive on Friday."

And the Lord God said, "How about the unicorns and the fowls of the air, by sevens?"

And Noah wrung his hands and wept, saying, "Lord, unicorns are a discontinued line; thou canst not find them anywhere. And fowls of the air are sold only in half-dozen lots. Lord, Lord, thou knowest how it is."

And the Lord in his wisdom said, "Noah, my son, I knowest. Why else dost thou think I would cause a flood to descend upon the earth?"

36. WHAT CAN I DO FOR MY CHURCH?

I can be sympathetic with its ideals.

I can be loyal to its services of worship.

I can uphold it in prayer.

I can contribute toward its support.

I can aid in its ministry.

I can welcome guests to the services.

I can promote good fellowship.

I can seek out and help the discouraged.

I can refrain from criticism.

I can invite my friends and neighbors.

I can help create a spiritual atmosphere.

I can encourage the study of God's Word.

I can dedicate my talents to God's service.

I can be kind and courteous to all.

I can see the best in my fellow church members.

37. MR. M. T. BENCH

Mr. M. T. Bench is an unwelcome visitor, but he always attends church — except on Easter Sunday and maybe Mother's Day. He likes to sit up front, which is more than you can say for most of our church members.

On wet, cold, or hot Sundays — and especially at evening services — he brings all his relatives and at some of our special meetings he even brings his neighbors.

His favorite place is near the pulpit. With never a change of expression, he tries to stare the preacher out of the pulpit. He is as responsive as a tombstone.

He is apparently deaf, for he hears nothing the minister says. I am sure he is mute, for he doesn't sing or pray or speak to his neighbor in a friendly manner.

What can we do with him? He doesn't like crowds, so he stays away from church when our members fill the pews. Let's get rid of this embarrassing fellow. Maybe if you come to church, Mr. M. T. Bench will stay home.

38. NOT ON SUNDAY NIGHT

I love the church that Jesus bought,
  And know that it is right;
I go there on Sunday morning,
  But not on Sunday night.

I love to sing the songs of God,
  Such worship must be right;
This I do on Sunday morn,
  But not on Sunday night.

I love to hear the gospel, too,
  It gives me pure delight;
I hear it Sunday morning,
  But not on Sunday night.

God bless our forward-moving church,
  And give it power and might;
And let it march on Sunday morning,
  But not on Sunday night!

—Author unknown

39. YOUR VERY OWN ROUND TUIT

ROUND
TUIT

At last we have obtained a supply of round tuits so we can include one in each copy of our church newsletter this issue.

Please clip it out and save it. It's a valuable piece of merchandise.

Some church members have been saying, "I will start going to church, or tithing, or singing in the church choir, just as soon as I get a round tuit. Now you have your very own round tuit, and you can do all those things you've been intending to do. With your round tuit in hand, you'll certainly want to get more involved in the life of your church.

40. A SAD ANNOUNCEMENT

7/14/85

With great regret we announce the loss of one of our church's most valuable families. Mr. and Mrs. Someone Else have moved away. The vacancy they have left will be hard to fill. The Else family had been with us for many years. They did far more than their share of work around the church.

Whenever there was a job to do, a class to teach, or a meeting to arrange or attend, their name was on everyone's list: "Let Someone Else do it." Whenever visitation was mentioned, this wonderful family was looked to for inspiration as well as results: "Someone Else will bring people to church." Mr. and Mrs. Else were also the biggest givers in the church: "Let Someone Else make up the difference."

The Someone Else family were wonderful people, but they were only human. They could spread themselves only so far. They did the best they could, but people expected too much from them.

Now Mr. and Mrs. Else are gone. They left us a wonderful example, but who will follow it? Who is going to do the things that Someone Else did?

41. EMPOWERED BY THE HOLY SPIRIT

Let me tell you about a church that had some real problems; but in spite of all of these reached thousands of people for Christ.

It was located in the wrong place. Most of the people looked on the members of this church with scorn and ridicule.

This church didn't have a building in which to meet. It was poor. Most of the members were on the verge of poverty.

The members of the church weren't trained for their jobs.

Their membership was small — only about 120.

The treasurer had just run off with the church's money.

The chief leader of this church had a way of putting his foot in his mouth. He was constantly making people mad.

There were divisions among the members of this church. Several were forced to flee to other cities because of persecution.

The one thing this church had going for it was the power of the Holy Spirit. It was the church in Jerusalem, described in the Book of Acts. With all its problems, this church baptized 3,000 people after its first revival service!

42. WHAT MAKES A CHURCH GROW?

According to church growth specialists, at least ten factors must be present in a church before it will grow. How do you think our church measures up in the following areas?

1. We must create a climate of happiness in the church. People must enjoy coming to a church before it will grow.

2. There must be a loving climate. God has given the world the right to judge the church by how we love one another.

3. The church that would grow must have a Bible-centered atmosphere.

4. The members of the church must be enthusiastic.

5. There should be freedom rather than formality in the operation of the church. A relaxed atmosphere is essential for meaningful worship, Bible study, and fellowship.

6. The growing church is evangelistic. It must be zealous to win lost people to Christ.

7. A growing church is an authoritarian church. Its authority comes from God.

8. In order to grow, a church must be daring. It must be will-

ing to attempt daring and different programs and methods of reaching people.

9. A growing church has a great faith. Its members have vision and the faith to make that vision into reality.

10. A growing church is a praying church. We would be better at talking to people about God if we were more faithful at talking to God about people.

43. YOU ARE IMPORTANT

Xvxn though my typxwritxr is an old modxl, it works quitx wxll xxcxpt for onx of thx kxys. I'vx wishxd many timxs that it workxd pxrfxctly. Trux, thxrx arx forty-two kxys functioning wxll xnough, but just onx kxy not working makxs thx diffxr-xncx.

Somxtimxs, it sxxms to mx that our church is somxwhat likx my typxwritxr—not all thx kxy pxoplx arx working propxrly. You may say, "Wxll, I'm only onx pxrson. It won't makx much diffxrxncx." But thx church, to bx xfficixnt, nxxds thx activx participation of xvxry pxrson.

Thx nxxt timx you think your xfforts arxn't nxxdxd, rxmxm-bxr my typxwritxr, and say to yoursxlf, "I'm a kxy pxrson and I'm nxxdxd vxry much."

44. DIFFERENT PEWS

In most churches the pews look alike. But they are really very different.

The critical pew. This pew watches the minister of the church with an eagle eye. The singing is too soft or too loud. The building is always too hot or too cold. The critical pew finds everything but the blessing of God.

The irregular pew. Sometimes the irregular pew is full; some-times it's empty. The problem is, you never know what to ex-pect from this pew.

The cordial pew. This pew is always radiant like the sunshine. This pew greets other pews with genuine cordiality, extends a handshake to every visitor, and listens with joy to the sermon.

The prayerful pew. This pew spends a moment or two with bowed head in silent prayer on entering the church. This pew comes to worship, and brings the spirit of worship with it into the church.

Which of these pews will you occupy when you come to worship in the Lord's house next Sunday?

45. A LITTLE PUSH

I was sitting in my car the other day when an old clunker stalled nearby. The driver was unable to start the old car, and traffic quickly started backing up behind him. Horns sounded and angry drivers shouted their unpleasant words at the embarrassed man. After a while, cars began to pull around the old car. Finally, one person drove up behind the stalled vehicle and gave it a push. Soon it began moving under its own power and traffic got underway again.

How like life that is! Someone is halted by circumstances. Most people shout their disgust at the unfortunate person and leave him to his fate. All he really needs is a little push to get started again.

Just as in any church, we have a few "stalled vehicles" who need a little push to get on the move again. If you know of someone who is losing interest in the church, or someone who is mired up to his axles in personal problems, offer him a little encouragement.

46. THE MEASURE OF TRUE GREATNESS

A church is great in the sight of God only when it is:

Great in spirit. The warmth of fellowship is apparent to all who worship in a great church.

Great in love. Its love abounds toward all sinners. The members love one another with real devotion.

Great in compassion. Its heart reaches out to those who need its ministry. Only by having a compassionate heart can a church be great.

Great in Christian living. Its members live a dedicated Christian life. It has no place for worldliness.

Great in loyalty. Its members are loyal to the Lord and his church through their dedication of time, talent, and money to his service.

47. I VOTED TO CLOSE THE CHURCH

Last Sunday I voted to close the church — not maliciously but thoughtlessly.

I voted to close its doors so its witness and testimony would be stopped. I voted to close the Bible on the pulpit — the Bible given to us by the blood of martyrs. I voted for our minister to stop preaching the truths of the gospel. I voted that children no longer be taught the stories of the Bible and the songs of salvation and God's love.

I voted that the voice of the choir and congregation be hushed, no more to sing the great hymns of the church. I voted for every missionary to be called home. I voted for the darkness of superstition, the degrading influence of sin, the blight of ignorance, and the curse of selfishness.

I could have gone to church last Sunday, but I didn't. I stayed away. By my laxity and indifference, I voted to close the church.

48. TEN COMMANDMENTS OF A FRIENDLY CHURCH

1. Speak to people, even if you don't know their names. There is nothing as nice or cheerful as a friendly word of greeting.

2. Smile at people. It takes seventy-two muscles to frown and only fourteen to smile. Your smile is one of your finest assets. Use it regularly.

3. Call people by name. The sweetest music to any person's ears is the sound of his own name.

4. Be friendly and helpful. If you want a friend, be one.

5. Be cordial. Speak and act as if everything you do is a genuine pleasure. Try to look happy, and you'll be happy.

6. Be genuinely interested in people. If you try, you can like everybody. Don't limit yourself to a few friends when there are so many likable people all around you.

7. Be generous with praise and sparing with criticism.

8. Be considerate of the feelings of others.

9. Watch for ways to serve others. What we do for others counts most in life.

10. Add to all of these a good sense of humor, a generous dose of patience, and a dash of humility.

Are you doing all you can to make your church a friendly church? If not, why not start today?

4
Sentence
Sermons

---

49. WISE PEOPLE

We all admire the wisdom of those people who come to us for advice.

50. DON'T SAY IT

There's nothing wrong with having nothing to say—unless you insist on saying it.

51. NO TIME LEFT

Give your time to improving yourself, and you'll have little time left for criticizing others.

52. WALL BUILDERS

People are lonely because they build walls instead of bridges.

53. DESTINATION: ANYWHERE

The person who doesn't know where he's going usually gets there in record time.

54. FAITH UNLOCKS

Prayer is the key to heaven, but faith unlocks the door.

55. A HAPPY MARRIAGE

A happy marriage exists when the couple is as deeply in love as it is in debt!

1/20/85 Insert Sor bulletin
56. PLAN AHEAD

Plan ahead. It wasn't raining when Noah built the ark.

57. GOOD TIMING

Statistics prove that the best time to buy anything is a year ago.

58. NO FREE RIDE

If you get something for a song, watch out for the accompaniment.

59. THE BURDEN WE DON'T MIND

Money is one burden most of us are willing to shoulder.

60. DRESSING UP THE TRUTH

The naked truth is always easier to take when it comes dressed in a smile.

61. THE SHADOW

Worry always gives a little thing a big shadow.

62. IF AT FIRST . . .

If at first you don't succeed, you'll get plenty of advice.

63. TOUGH GRASS

The greener grass next door is probably just as hard to cut.

64. EASY TO FIND

Fault is the easiest thing in the world to find.

65. MODESTY FOR EVERYONE

Everyone has something to be modest about.

66. UNDERCOVER OPPORTUNITY

The trouble with opportunity is it always comes disguised as hard work.

67. DO IT NOW!

Today is seldom too early; tomorrow is usually too late.

68. HAPPY SAVER

The happiest miser on earth is one who saves friends.

69. TALKED INTO A CORNER

A loose tongue often gets its owner into a tight place.

70. NO LATE PAYMENTS

The wages of sin are always paid on time.

71. DON'T STOP SHORT

Charity begins at home, but it shouldn't stop there.

72. HOW TO LOSE FRIENDS

One sure way to lose friends is to win all the arguments.

73. WAITING ON GOD

It's good to wait on the Lord — as long as you're busy while you wait.

74. NO COMPETITION

Making an honest living should be easy; there's so little competition these days.

75. THE LADDER BARRIER

All that stands between some people and the top of the ladder is the ladder.

76. SUCCESS AND HAPPINESS

Success is getting what you want; happiness is wanting what you get.

77. A HARD THING TO DO

One of the hard things about business is minding your own.

78. A SURE SIGN OF FAILURE

A person hasn't failed until he begins to blame someone else for his failure.

79. THE KNOCKS THAT HURT

Hard knocks won't hurt you — unless you are doing the knocking.

80. ROSES IN DECEMBER

God gave us memories so we could have roses in December.

81. DROPPING A CONVERSATION

It's all right to hold a conversation, but you should let go of it now and then.

82. CONCRETE MINDS

Some minds are like concrete—all mixed up and permanently set.

83. NO COMPLIMENT

Remember the time when "sound as a dollar" was a compliment?

84. WATCH YOUR PRAYERS

Don't pray for rain if you intend to complain about the mud.

85. THE BEST HELPING HAND

The best kind of helping hand is the one at the end of your arm.

86. MEDIUM OF EXCHANGE?

It's true that money is a medium of exchange—a medium amount of it won't exchange for very much these days.

87. PLENTY OF LAUGHS

If we learn to laugh at ourselves, we will always have something to make us happy.

88. PRESCRIPTION FOR WORRY

Blessed is the person who is too busy to worry during the day and too sleepy to worry at night.

42

89. HOW TO SHORTEN THE WINTER

The best way to make the winter short is to borrow some money you have to pay back in the spring.

90. CLOSING THE DISTANCE

Laughter is the shortest distance between two people.

91. MODESTY IS . . .

Modesty is the art of encouraging others to find out for themselves how important you are.

92. TEMPER AND PRIDE

Temper gets most of us in trouble, and pride keeps us there.

93. DEFINITION OF AN EXPERT

An expert is an ordinary person a hundred miles from home.

94. A PERFECT GUEST

A perfect guest always makes his host feel right at home.

95. FROM THE SIDELINES

It's always easy to see both sides of an issue you're not particularly concerned about.

96. THE LOUD SOUNDS OF NOTHING

The less some people know, the more anxious they are to tell you about it!

97. NEVER TOO BUSY

A person is never too busy to stop and tell you how busy he is.

98. TOO MUCH WORK

Work is a fine thing if it doesn't take too much of your leisure time.

99. A NICE GUY

A nice guy is a person who never heard the story before.

100. INFLATIONARY LESSON

Every time history repeats itself, the price of the lesson goes up.

101. CHARACTER'S HOLDING POWER

Ability may get you to the top, but only character will keep you there.

102. FRUSTRATION IS . . .

Frustration is not having anyone to blame but yourself.

103. WHEN TO STOP TALKING

Always try to stop talking before people stop listening.

104. BLISTERS PEOPLE

Some people are like blisters; they never show up until after the work is done.

105. THE BUSIEST DAY

If tomorrow ever got here, it would be the busiest day of the year.

106. DIGGING OR JUMPING?

Digging for the facts is better than jumping to conclusions.

107. KNOWLEDGE THAT COUNTS

It's what we learn after we think we know it all that really counts.

108. STOP ME, LORD

Lord, fill my mouth with worthwhile stuff,
And stop me when I've said enough.

2/85 109. LEARN FROM OTHERS

Learn from the mistakes of others. You won't live long enough to make them all yourself.

110. ARGUING THE ISSUE

Arguing about religion is much easier than practicing it.

111. A TENNIS VIEW OF LIFE

Life is like tennis; the player who serves well has a good chance of winning.

112. NO SUBSTITUTE FOR EXPERIENCE

There's nothing like experience; it helps you recognize a mistake the second time you make it.

113. HOW TO KILL TIME

The best way to kill time is to work it to death.

114. THE POWER OF A WHISPER

If you can't get people to listen any other way, tell them it's confidential.

115. SOME PEOPLE!

Some people have the nerve to go right on talking when you're interrupting.

116. GRAND CENTRAL STATION

A hospital room is a place where friends of the patient go to talk to other friends of the patient.

117. GOOD ADVICE

If you ask enough people, you'll usually find someone who advises you to do exactly what you planned to do in the first place.

5
Prayer

118. THE MINISTRY OF PRAYER

There's a holy high vocation
Needing workers everywhere;
'Tis the highest form of service—
'Tis the ministry of prayer.

None need stand idly longing
For a place in which to share
Active service for the Master—
There's always room in prayer.

In these days of tribulation,
Wickedness pervades the air;
And the battles we engage in
Must be won by fervent prayer.

There's no weapon half so mighty
As what the intercessors bear;
Nor a broader field of service
Than the ministry of prayer.

—A. S. Woolworth

119. THANK YOU, LORD, FOR SAYING "NO"

Lord, thank you for not answering all my prayers. All my life I've prayed for special favors. I've pestered you for many things which weren't worthy of your attention. I've asked you to solve problems of my own creation that I should solve myself. I have prayed that you would make life easy for me. I have asked you to help me answer questions which I ought to answer by working and thinking for myself.

I have prayed for sure ways to success and short cuts to wealth when I should have been working to attain goals that really satisfy. I have asked for good health instead of exercising my body and being more careful about my diet and health habits. I have asked you to help me understand my fellow man when I should have been listening and trying to help him with his problems.

I realize now that if you had answered all my prayers, I would be weak, dependent, and lazy. By forcing me to work out some of my own problems, you have helped me to become strong. Now I face the world with the belief that it can be conquered and there is reason to "be of good cheer."

You have helped me to become a person I can respect. My days are full of opportunity to help others. That's the most important thing I could have prayed for. So thank you, Lord, for helping me to become the person you knew I could become — not by giving me my every wish but by refusing to answer some of my prayers in the way I wanted them answered.

120. SIGNS OF ANSWERED PRAYER

If you rise from prayer forgiven and clean inside, prayer has been answered.

If you rise more conscious of God's greatness, goodness, mercy, love, and nearness, prayer has been answered.

If you rise with greater love and compassion for other people, answered prayer is transforming your selfish nature.

If you rise with an abiding sense of peace in spite of the great problems that beset your life, God has answered by preparing you to confront these difficulties.

If you rise with clearer vision, greater purpose, a more positive outlook, renewed strength, and fresh inspiration, rest assured that your prayer has been answered.

121. THE SECRET OF THE BENDED KNEE

Have you ever watched a bird sleeping on its perch and never falling off? How does it manage to do this?

The secret is the tendons of the bird's legs. They are so constructed that when the leg is bent at the knee, the claws contract and grip like a steel trap. The claws refuse to let go until the knees are unbent again. The bended knee gives the bird the ability to hold on to his perch so tightly.

Isn't this also the secret of the holding power of the Christian? Daniel found this to be true. Surrounded by a pagan environment, tempted to compromise with evil, urged to weaken his grip on God, he refused to let go. He held firm when others faltered because he was a man of prayer. He knew the power of the bended knee.

From sleeping birds we can learn the secret of holding things which are most precious to us — honestly, purity, thoughtfulness, honor, character. That secret is the knee bent in prayer, seeking to get a firmer grip on those values which make life worth living. When we hold firmly to God in prayer, we can rest assured he will hold tightly to us.

—Rollin S. Burhans

6
Sunday School
Attendance and Support

122. THREE GOOD REASONS FOR SUNDAY SCHOOL

1. **Bible study.** Feeding on the Word of God is just as essential to the Christian's spiritual growth as food is to physical growth.

2. **Evangelism.** The Sunday School is the arm of the church that leads in reaching people for Christ and the church.

3. **Application.** One important objective of the Sunday School is to lead members not only to understand the message of the Bible but to see how it applies to their daily lives.

123. A SUNDAY SCHOOL TEACHER'S PRAYER

A sculptor took a piece of clay
And molded perfectly
The figure of a little child,
So beautiful to see;
But when I held it in my hand,
No warmth of life was there—

Its cold, unchanging beauty
  Was all that it could share.

God sent a little child to me
  So I could supervise
The teaching that would satisfy
  The wonder in his eyes;
And when I took his little hand
  To guide him on his way,
I felt the warmth of trust and love
  He shares with me each day.

And so, dear Lord, I come to thee
  In all humility,
To ask for wisdom, strength, and love
  That I may always be
The kind of teacher who can help
  In some kind, loving way,
To mold a better, stronger child
  With every passing day.

—Harold H. LeCrone

124. A JUDGE'S HAUNTING WORDS

I went to Sunday school when I was small and learned all about God. After I was married I decided to go again and take my children. I couldn't persuade my husband to go, but the children and I went regularly for a year. Then I skipped a Sunday. And soon I skipped two or three. Then we went only on special days. Soon I joined a bowling team that competed on Sunday. I could go to church and Sunday school, but I would have to give up my bowling. Bowling won the battle.

Not long ago in a courtroom I heard a judge say, "Twenty years!" He was pronouncing sentence on my 21-year-old son— a punishment for a robbery which ended in the death of a man. The sentence might have been less, but my son took a sneering, defiant attitude all through the trial, ridiculing every officer and official in the courtroom.

But the crowning, shocking climax came when the judge stern-ly asked, "Young man, don't you believe in God?"

51

My son laughed and said, "God? Who's that?" Every person in the courtroom turned to look at me. If only I had those years to live over! I would attend Sunday school and church faithfully and make sure my children attended as well.

125. SUNDAY SCHOOL WORKER'S MEETING

A salesman doesn't skip sales meetings because he's experienced at his job.

A football player doesn't break training because he's a star!

A mechanic returns to the automobile factory periodically to learn about the latest models.

And a doctor uses the latest drugs and the most modern techniques available.

Can Sunday school workers afford to neglect their regularly scheduled meetings? These meetings are designed to make you more effective leaders in your Sunday school. Don't forsake this important part of your work.

126. THE BUILDER

A builder built a temple,
*   He wrought with grace and skill;*
Foundation, pillars, arches,
*   All fashioned to work his will.*

Men said, as they saw its beauty,
*   "Magnificent it is, my friend,*
Great is thy skill, O builder—
*   Thy fame shall never end!"*

A teacher built a temple
*   With loving and infinite care,*
Planning each arch with patience,
*   Laying each stone with prayer.*

None praised her unceasing efforts,
*   None knew of her wondrous plan,*
For the temple she was building
*   Was unseen by the eyes of man.*

Gone is the builder's temple,
Crumpled into the dust;
Low lies each stately pillar,
Food for consuming rust.

But the temple the teacher fashioned
Will last while the ages roll,
For that beautiful, unseen temple
Was a child's immortal soul.

—Author unknown

127. SUNDAY SCHOOL: WHO NEEDS IT?

Since many church members never attend Sunday school, the "who needs it" question deserves attention. Just to get this question in focus, let's assume the church has no Sunday school. What difference would it make?

1. If we didn't have a Sunday school, there would be no systematic approach to teaching persons of all ages the Word of God.

2. If we didn't have a Sunday school, there would be no concerted effort to reach persons who are outside the influence of the church.

3. If we didn't have a Sunday school, there would be less continuing opportunity for a significant number of our members to use their talents for God.

4. If we didn't have a Sunday school, there would be no formal Christian influence on members and prospects.

5. If we didn't have a Sunday school, there would be no serious attempt to involve large numbers of people in Christian worship.

6. If we didn't have a Sunday school, there would be no effective avenue for providing a continuous witness to lost people.

7. If we didn't have a Sunday school, there would be no consistent way to instruct and enlist our members in the stewardship principle of life.

8. If we didn't have a Sunday school, there would be no specific process for the Christian nurture and growth of our children and youth.

9. If we didn't have a Sunday school, there would be no practical means for helping adults grow in spiritual and emotional maturity.

10. If we didn't have a Sunday school, we would have to create an organization similar to the Sunday school to enable our church to do its work more effectively.

128. DADDY HAD A LITTLE BOY

Daddy had a little boy,
  His soul was white as snow;
He never went to Sunday school
  'Cause Daddy wouldn't go.

He never heard the Word of God
  That thrills the childish mind—
While other children went to class,
  This child was left behind.

As he grew from babe to youth,
  Dad saw to his dismay,
A soul that once was snowy white
  Become a dingy gray.

Dad even started back to church
  And Bible study, too;
He begged the pastor, "Isn't there
  A thing that you can do?"

The preacher tried and tried, and said,
  "We're just too far behind;
I tried to tell you years ago,
  But you would pay no mind."

And so another soul was lost,
  That once was white as snow;
Sunday school would have helped,
  But Daddy wouldn't go.

—Author unknown

129. WHY I ATTEND SUNDAY SCHOOL

I attend Sunday school because:

The best book is studied and taught. I want to know and follow this book in my daily life.

The best day of the week is observed. I want to keep the Lord's day holy.

The best people are assembled for Sunday school, and I desire the blessing of their friendship and fellowship.

The best institution is alert and at work for the Master. I ought to invest myself where I will do my best for Christ and the church.

The best development as a Christian is attained through Sunday school. I want to continue to grow and develop as a follower of Christ.

130. INVOLVEMENT IS THE KEY

The secret of building a dynamic and growing Sunday school is packed into one word: *Involvement.* Here are three ways you can get your class members more involved in Sunday school.

1. Get them involved in the lesson. You as a teacher probably spend hours gathering maps, pictures, historical facts, and materials to use in presenting the lesson. Assign as many of these tasks as you can to other class members.

2. Get them involved in visiting absentees and prospects. A teacher can't afford to keep all the pleasures of visiting to himself. Get your class members involved in this task.

3. Get them involved in praying. Unite your class in daily prayer for lost people and others who need prayer. Lead them to discover the power of prayer in their lives. Don't be timid about having a spontaneous prayer meeting when urgent matters need prayer.

131. HOW A SUNDAY SCHOOL GROWS

1. Classes usually reach their maximum growth or saturation point within a few months after they are started.

2. The rate of growth of a class depends on the ability of the teacher, the activity of the class officers, and the spirit of the class.

3. New classes must be started regularly to make continuous growth possible.

4. New classes grow faster, reach more unsaved people, provide more workers, and encourage exciting classes to grow.

5. Age-basis grading offers the most logical plan for starting new classes.

6. Promotion from class to class recognizes the natural laws of growth, development, and advancement.

7. Adults must be brought to Sunday school through personal enlistment and visitation.

8. The rooms and equipment set the pattern for growth and efficiency.

9. Classes which meet individual spiritual needs through real Bible study, genuine Christian fellowship, and opportunities for service grow consistently in enrollment and attendance.

10. Classes with an evangelistic spirit grow more rapidly.

7
Visitation, Witnessing, and Christian Outreach

---

132. HOW JESUS REACHED PEOPLE

The tenth chapter of Luke shows us some of the methods Jesus used to enlist people in his kingdom. Perhaps we can use some of these methods today to reach lost people.

He sent out persons two-by-two to do person-to-person visitation.

He instructed these visitors to pray for other visitors to be sent forth so even more people could be reached.

He warned these visitors that the work would be difficult and that some people wouldn't listen.

Notice that these people whom Jesus sent out two-by-two weren't salaried employees.

Jesus commanded these people to go into the homes of their neighbors and friends and give their testimony.

Today there are still people who need to be reached for Christ and his church. Plan to share in this important outreach mission through your church.

133. WHAT IS EVANGELISM?

Evangelism is the sob of God over lost people.

It is the anguished cry of Jesus as he weeps over a doomed city.

It is the cry of Paul for the salvation of his kinsmen and countrymen.

It is the heart-wringing plea of Moses for God to spare his people.

It is the cry of John Knox, "Give me Scotland or I die."

It is the declaration of John Wesley, "The world is my parish."

It is the prayer of Billy Sunday, "Make me a giant for God."

It is the sob of parents in the night, weeping over a wayward child.

It is the secret of every great church.

—William T. Hall

134. HOW PEOPLE CHOOSE A CHURCH

A survey was taken among a group of suburban churches in one large city. Each church member interviewed was asked, "Why did you choose to join the particular church where you are now worshiping?"

Nine percent said they chose their church because of its architectural beauty.

Fourteen percent joined a church because of denominational loyalty.

Eighteen percent joined because it was convenient to their homes.

Three percent joined because of the influence of the pastor.

Twenty-two percent joined because there were people in the church whom they respected.

Thirty-four percent joined because neighbors or friends invited them to that church.

These statistics show that God is still using people to bring other people into the fellowship of his churches. How long has it been since you invited someone or offered to pick up someone and bring him to church?

Watch your community and neighborhood for newcomers. Get acquainted with them, and ask about their church affiliation. Invite them to your church.

135. THE RESULTS OF FAITHFUL WITNESSING

A boy gave his lunch to Jesus — and five thousand people were fed.

A slave girl spoke to her mistress about God — and her master, healed of his leprosy, became a devout believer.

Andrew told Peter about Jesus — and three years later Peter preached a sermon that was instrumental in bringing three thousand people into the church.

A Sunday school teacher visited Dwight Moody in the shop where he worked — and Moody became a famous evangelist who led thousands to the cross of Jesus Christ.

A little group of students met to pray for the lands where the gospel had never been heard — and the great movement of American foreign missions was launched.

Faithful witnessing can produce tremendous results. Tell someone about Jesus — and leave the results up to God.

136. WHAT IS A REVIVAL?

What is a real revival? A true revival is a rediscovery of the meaning of God in human experience. This includes genuine repentance of sin, vital faith in Christ, complete surrender to his cross, renewed enthusiasm about his kingdom, and a restless urge to win others to his will and way for their lives.

A real revival is a spiritual awakening that is pure in motive, sane in method, and permanent and creative in content. It is an earnest reasoning together about our hopes and fears. It is the soul's deep answer to the call of God. It is the wandering child's return to his spiritual roots.

A revival like this doesn't begin with someone else. It begins with each one of us. We who are Christians must humble ourselves and turn to God in repentance and faith.

137. WHAT VISITATION DOES

Vitalizes the work of the church.

Increases enrollment.

Secures cooperation between church and home.

Inspires regular attendance.

Typifies the spirit of Christ.

Affords soul-winning opportunities.

Touches the person far away from Christ.

Insures your own spiritual growth.

Obeys the command of Christ.

Nurtures friendships with new people.

138. WHEN IS REVIVAL OVER?

Revival is never completed:

If we place Christ first in our lives.

If we continue to share Christ with others.

If we continue to pray for our church leaders and our church programs.

If our leaders, teachers, and workers take their responsibilities seriously as a direct commission from God.

If we perform our responsibilities seriously and faithfully.

If we approach our church work with renewed enthusiasm and commitment.

139. DEFINITIONS OF COMMITMENT

Commitment is:

Sunday school workers visiting in the homes of unsaved parents.

Parents and children making sure the way of Christ is made plain at home through word and example.

A high school student looking for unsaved teenagers among the hundreds he sees at school each day.

A church member willing to visit for the church and for Christ.

Neighbors inviting unsaved friends for coffee and for conversation which gets around to spiritual matters.

A teacher leading his class to visit, to care, and to minister to others.

A church member praying daily about an indifferent friend.

A Christian couple cultivating new friendships for Christ.

Every church member finding a place of service in the church and putting Christ first in all of life.

140. THE SECRET OF SUCCESSFUL WITNESSING

Successful witnessing depends on several things:

1. The joy you have in your own heart. If you are thrilled to be a Christian, you won't have trouble convincing lost people of the value of accepting Christ as Savior.

2. The purity of your own life. If your own life is right with God, lost people will listen to what you have to say. If your life is tainted with sin, your testimony for Christ will be weak.

3. Your ability to use the Bible. The successful Christian witness has to know his Bible. Without a thorough knowledge of God's Word, you won't be able to answer the questions and excuses thrown at you by the unsaved.

4. Your willingness to try. You can't win others to Christ if you don't make the effort! Catch the vision. Talk about Jesus to everyone you meet. Winning others to Christ is one of the greatest joys in life.

5. Your ability to get a clear commitment. Many people can present the way of salvation to a sinner, but they fail when it comes to getting a definite decision. Deal with people with a sense of urgency. Press for a clear decision for Christ.

141. NEEDED: LOYALTY DURING THE REVIVAL

A church has no greater need than loyal members who will support the revival services. Here are some ways this loyalty will be expressed:

1. Remarks of praise and appreciation about the church and its workers.

2. Prompt and regular attendance at all services.

3. Faithfulness to any task to which one is assigned.

4. Generous financial support of the church and the revival.

5. Willingness to adopt and accept the total revival program sponsored by the church.

6. Consistent living that honors Christ and his teachings.

7. Tolerance toward those with whom we disagree.

8. Humility that serves gladly in the place of greatest need.

142. PORTRAIT OF A PROSPECT

Prospects aren't strange creatures whom someone else finds and reports to the church. Prospects are real live people whom you meet every day. The supermarket clerk, the beautician, the bank teller, the school teacher, the close, personal friend — all these may be people whom our church should reach with the gospel.

A prospect is a person who needs Jesus Christ as Savior. This includes everyone within the range of your witness who is not a Christian. Another type of prospect is a Christian who has moved to your community and who needs a church home.

A prospect is someone you know — not just any man, woman, or teenager — but a person with a name, feelings, and identity.

Do you know a prospect? Witness to him. Try to reach him for Jesus Christ and the church.

143. THE MASTER KEY

Most large buildings have keys for every door in the building.

But there is usually one key which fits every door. It's called the master key.

In a church there are many keys to various activities and ministries. But there is one key which fits everything. It's called visitation.

Visitation is the key to Sunday school growth. It's the key to revival, evangelistic outreach, and successful soul-winning. Visitation is the keynote in our Lord's commission, "Go ye into all the world and preach the gospel."

144. A LASTING REVIVAL

Thou hast revived thy people, Lord,
In the glorious days just past!
We have felt thy wondrous power,
And our hearts ask, "Will it last?"

It will last if we continue
As did thy disciples of old,
Steadfast in prayer and service,
Winning others to thy fold.

Studying daily thy blessed Word,
Having fellowship deep and sweet,
Exalting Jesus, our blessed Lord,
Laying our gifts at his feet.

Heaven's revival glow will stay
If we continue in his way!

—Author unknown

8
The Centrality
of Christ

---

145. JESUS MY ALL

Christ my Savior, Christ my friend,
Christ my treasure without end;
Christ when waves of sorrow roll,
Christ the comfort of my soul.

Christ when all around should fail,
Christ when enemies prevail;
Christ when false accusers rise,
Christ my solace in the skies.

Christ when days are dark and drear,
Christ when all around is clear;
Christ when all the earth is gone,
Christ my portion on the throne.

Christ at home and Christ abroad,
Christ my company on the road;
Christ in sickness, Christ in health,
Christ in poverty and wealth.

Christ who once on earth has trod,
Christ the blessed Son of God;
Christ for now and Christ for then,
Christ my Savior and my friend.

—Author unknown

146. JESUS IS ABLE

He is able to save. Hebrews 7:25.

He is able to keep you from falling. Jude 24.

He is able to help those who are tempted. 1 Corinthians 10:13.

He is able to do for us more than we ask or think. Ephesians 3:20.

He is able to make all grace abound. 2 Corinthians 9:8.

147. WHAT JESUS MEANS TO OTHERS

To the artist Jesus Christ is the one altogether lovely.

To the architect he is the chief cornerstone.

To the baker he is the living bread.

To the banker he is the hidden treasure.

To the biologist he is the life.

To the builder he is the sure foundation.

To the doctor he is the great physician.

To the educator he is the master teacher.

To the farmer he is the sower and the lord of the harvest.

To the florist he is the rose of Sharon and the lily of the valley.

To the geologist he is the rock of ages.

To the horticulturist he is the true vine.

To the judge he is the righteous judge of all mankind.

To the juror he is the faithful and true witness.

To the jeweler he is the pearl of great price.

To the lawyer he is the counselor and the lawgiver.

To the newspaper reporter he is the Good News.

To the philanthropist he is the unspeakable gift.

To the philosopher he is the wisdom of God.

To the preacher he is the Word of God.

To the sculptor he is the living stone.

To the servant he is the good master.

To the statesman he is the lord of all nations.

To the student he is the living truth.

To the theologian he is the author and finisher of our faith.

To the sinner he is the Lamb of God that takes away the sin of the world.

To the Christian he is the Son of the living God, the Savior, Redeemer, and Lord.

148. JESUS ESSENTIAL FOR ETERNAL LIFE

A person can go to heaven without health, wealth, fame, learning, culture, or beauty. But he can't go to heaven without Christ. Jesus said, "I am the way, the truth, and the life; no man cometh unto the Father, but by me" (John 14:6).

1/13/95   149. THE CHRISTIAN'S RICHES

In Christ we have:

A love that can never be fathomed.

A life that can never die.

A peace that can never be understood.

A rest that can never be disturbed.

A joy that can never be diminished.

A hope that can never be disappointed.

A glory that can never be clouded.

A happiness that can never be interrupted.

A light that can never be extinguished.

A strength that can never be overcome.

A beauty that can never be marred.

A purity that can never be defiled.

Resources that can never be exhausted.

150. JESUS OUR STANDARD

Bushels, pounds, rods, and dollars. Without universally accepted standards like these, we would have chaos in the business world. And it is just as necessary to have standards in the spiritual side of life.

We do have Jesus' life as our standard of living. The highest ambition of every Christian should be to live as Jesus lived.

Is Jesus your standard in love?

Is Jesus your standard in forgiveness?

Is Jesus your standard in service?

Is Jesus your standard in kindness?

Is Jesus your standard in dealing with others?

9
Easter
Messages

---

151. PALM SUNDAY VICTORY

They cut the branches from the trees
And strewed them in the way,
Because they knew their Lord and King
Would come along that day.

They sang hosanna to the King
And praised his holy name—
Now even in this modern day,
We, too, should do the same.

The Christ who came that palm-strewn way
To enter in the gate,
Will enter in your heart today,
So do not make him wait.

That palm-strewn path of long ago
Is still a victory sign
That Christ still comes along the way
Into your heart and mine.

—Raymond Orner

152. THE CARPENTER OF GALILEE

The carpenter of Galilee
Comes down the street again,
In every land, in every age,
He still is calling men.

On any day we hear him knock—
He goes from door to door—
Are any workmen out of work?
The carpenter needs more.

—Hilda W. Smith

153. EASTER MEANS NEW LIFE

New life is what Easter is all about. Jesus Christ died and rose from the grave that you might have life beyond the grave and that you might have life in this world today—rich, full, and abundant life. Let Jesus come and live within your heart today.

"Behold, I stand at the door and knock" (Revelation 3:20).

"Christ in you, the hope of glory" (Colossians 1:27).

"He that abideth in me, and I in him, the same bringeth forth much fruit" (John 15:5).

Easter is a good time to start living!

154. HE IS RISEN!

How do I know that Christ is risen?
What proof have I to give?
He touched my life one blessed day
And I began to live.

How do I know he left the tomb
That morning long ago?
I met him just this morning
And my heart is still aglow.

How do I know that endless life
He gained for me that day?
His life within is proof enough
Of immortality.

How do I know that Christ still lives
Rich blessings to impart?
He walks with me along the way
And lives within my heart.

— Author unknown

155. THE VICTORIOUS MESSAGE OF EASTER

Easter points to one great event—the resurrection of Jesus Christ. Easter was God's vindication of our Lord's life and death. Jesus had endured anguish, agony, and death in the belief that God would not remain silent in the face of sin and injustice. Everything Jesus had taught about the real meaning of life was proven when God raised him from the dead.

The resurrection of Jesus speaks a victorious word to us today. In spite of our haunting questions and problems, Easter affirms the mighty truth that God lives in us and we in him. Easter brings us renewed assurance that God loves us with a love that is greater than any we can imagine.

May this Easter vision give us strength for victorious living every day of the year.

156. RESURRECTION LIVING

For resurrection living
There is resurrection power,
And the praise and prayer of trusting
May glorify each hour.

For common days are holy
And years an Easter-tide
To those who with the living Lord
In living faith abide.

— Author unknown

10
Home and
Family Life

157. HOW FAMILIES GROW SPIRITUALLY

You don't grow a Christian family by going through a daily
ritual. But neither do you grow one without planning and
definite cultivation. Here are some proven activities that help a
family to grow spiritually.

1. Worshiping together regularly.

2. Attending church together.

3. Giving thanks to God at mealtimes.

4. Having fun together.

5. Expressing love and affection openly and freely.

6. Undergirding and supporting one another.

7. Working together; accepting responsibility for doing chores
   and jobs around the house.

8. Reaching out to others as a Christian family.

158. MOTHERHOOD

Dear Christian mothers, sing your praise
Through all your busy, happy days
To God our Father, kind and good,
For all the joys of motherhood.

For that wee babe with smiling charm
That softly nestles on your arm;
For childish laughter gay and sweet,
And sounds of little scampering feet.

For that young precious merry mite
Who walks with hand in yours held tight;
And for the others older grown,
Who've learned to proudly walk alone.

For blessings—often mixed with tears—
As they mature through passing years;
And that deep joy that naught can dim,
When children give their hearts to him.

Fear not the coming day to face,
For God will give you strength and grace;
And hers shall be a great reward
Who trains her children for the Lord.

—Margaret K. Fraser

159. DEFINITIONS OF A CHRISTIAN FAMILY

A Christian family is one in which parents live the Christian life and practice the presence of God so their children come to accept God as the greatest reality of life.

A Christian family is one in which each member is accepted and respected as a person of sacred worth.

A Christian family is one that seeks to bring every member into the Christian way of living.

A Christian family is one that accepts the responsibility of worship and Christian instruction in order to develop the spiritual life of each person.

A Christian family is one that shows its faith in God, observes daily prayer, and offers thanks to God at mealtimes.

A Christian family is one that is committed to Christian behavior in the family, community, and world.

160. A FATHER'S EXAMPLE

6/15/85

There are little eyes upon you,
And they're watching night and day;
There are little ears that listen
To every word you say.

There are little hands all eager
To do the things you do;
And a little boy who's dreaming
Of the day he'll be like you.

You're the little fellow's idol,
You're the wisest of the wise;
In his little mind, about you
No suspicions ever rise.

He believes in you devoutly,
Holds that all you say and do
He will say and do in your way
When he's grown up just like you.

There's a wide-eyed little fellow
Who believes you're always right;
And his ears are always open
As he watches day and night.

You are setting an example
Every day in all you do,
For the little boy who's waiting
To grow up to be like you.

—Edgar A. Guest

161. GOD'S WILL IN OUR FAMILIES

Happy is the family that knows God's will. For the will of God is found in loving and helping one another — not in turning aside to admire God, while forgetting the people who are the crown of his creation.

God has given us the commandment that we should love one another, and this applies to the people who live at home with us. When we love one another, we are doing the will of God.

162. HOW PARENTS TEACH AT HOME

Are you a parent or a teacher to your children? To find out, complete this simple little questionnaire:

	YES	NO
1. Your friends and relatives point out that your son or daughter does some things "just like you."	_____	_____
2. Your child has at least one irritating habit that reminds your mother of the way you acted at the same age.	_____	_____
3. Your face has turned red more than once when your child repeated an opinion you had expressed at home—even though he didn't attribute the remark to you.	_____	_____
4. Your child takes most of your statements as fact, quoting you as an authority when playmates question his statements.	_____	_____
5. Your child reads aloud a statement from a book or paper and then asks you, "Is that true?"	_____	_____
6. Your child shows the same attitude you have toward such things as snakes, dogs, and dark corners.	_____	_____

Did you put a lot of checks in the "yes" column? If you did, it shows that parents really are teachers of their children. Spend some time thinking about the important things your children should be taught. Then determine to do a good job of communicating these truths to your children.

163. A MOTHER'S BEATITUDES

Blessed is the mother who understands her child, for she shall inherit a kingdom of memories.

Blessed is the mother who knows how to comfort, for she shall possess a child's devotion.

Blessed is the mother who guides by the path of righteousness, for she shall be proud of her children.

Blessed is the mother who is never shocked, for she shall receive and know confidence and security.

Blessed is the mother who teaches respect, for she shall be respected.

Blessed is the mother who emphasizes the good and minimizes the bad, for her children shall follow her example.

Blessed is the mother who answers questions honestly, for she shall always be trusted.

Blessed is the mother who treats her children as she would like to be treated, for her home shall always be filled with happiness.

164. CHILDREN LEARN WHAT THEY LIVE

If a child lives with criticism, he learns to condemn.

If he lives with hostility, he learns to fight.

If he lives with fear, he learns to be anxious and insecure.

If he lives with pity, he learns to feel sorry for himself.

If he lives with ridicule, he learns to be shy.

If he lives with shame, he learns to feel guilty.

If he lives with encouragement, he learns to be confident in himself and his abilities.

If he lives with tolerance, he learns to be tolerant of others.

If he lives with praise, he learns to be appreciative.

If he lives with acceptance, he learns to love.

If he lives with approval, he learns to like himself.

If he lives with recognition, he learns that it is good to set goals for himself.

If he lives with security, he learns to have faith in himself and in other people.

165. A MOTHER'S PRAYER

Make me a wise mother, O Lord. Keep me calm and give me patience to bear the small irritating things in life's daily routine.

Give me tolerance and understanding to bridge the gulf which exists between my generation and that of my children.

Help me to bear silently the physical and mental pain of those whom I love by reminding me that only through suffering may they understand the distress of others.

Let me be not too ready to guide my children's stumbling feet, but allow me to be ever near to bind up their bruises.

Give me a sense of humor that I may laugh with them but never at them.

Let me refrain from preaching with words. Keep me from forcing their confidences, but give me a sympathetic ear when they seek me out.

Help me to teach them that life must not be filled with compromises, but it should be replete with victories.

Keep my children close to me, O Lord, though miles may separate us. And let thy light so shine upon me that they, too, will see thy glory.

—Ruth Simrall Mackoy

166. MARRIAGE REQUIRES MATURITY

A successful marriage is not an accident. It is the result of hard work. It takes two people really trying to make a marriage succeed. The trying should begin before the "I do's," not after. Preparation involves two questions, "Am I ready for marriage?" and "How do I prepare for marriage?"

Some people think that age is the key to maturity. But age indicates very little. Some people are ready for marriage at an early age; others are not ready when they are thirty; and some never are. The real issue is not age but maturity. Successful marriages are built by mature people. Some signs of maturity in people are:

1. Accepting responsibility and then acting responsibly.

2. Learning to make independent, objective decisions on your own and in consultation with other people.

3. Living with the consequences of those decisions—refusing to pass the buck or to blame circumstances.

4. Giving as well as receiving.

5. Thinking of the needs of others.

6. Respecting the opinions of others and listening to them, although you may not agree with them.

7. Waiting for what you want—learning to postpone immediate gratification of needs and desires if greater good can be gained by waiting.

8. Learning not to take yourself too seriously.

9. Accepting help and advice from other people.

Evaluating your own maturity is never easy. But the best thing you can do for yourself and your future mate is to think about how mature you really are.

Marriage won't eliminate your personality hangups. It usually just makes them worse. If you are a reasonably mature person, you may be ready for marriage. If not, you owe it to yourself and the other person to wait until you are.

167. THE MEANEST MOTHER

I had the meanest mother in the world. While other kids ate candy for breakfast, I had to have cereal, eggs, and toast. When others had coke and candy for lunch, I had to eat a sandwich. As you can guess, my dinner was different from other kids'.

My mother insisted on knowing where I was at all times. She had to know who my friends were and what we were doing. She insisted that if I told her I would be gone an hour, I would be gone for an hour or less.

I'm ashamed to admit it, but she actually had the nerve to make us kids work. We had to wash dishes, make beds, and learn to cook. I believe she stayed awake at night, thinking up things for me to do!

By the time I became a teenager, she had grown even meaner. She embarrassed me by making my dates come to the front door to pick me up. And while my friends were dating at the mature ages of twelve and thirteen, my old-fashioned mother refused to let me date until I was sixteen.

In spite of the harsh way I was raised, I've never been arrested. And all my brothers and sisters turned out okay, too. I guess we owe it all to our mean mother. She insisted that we grow up into God-fearing, honest, responsible adults. I'm grateful to God that he gave me the meanest mother in the world!

168. THE TOUCH OF A BABY'S HAND

One little hand is lying
 So quietly on my breast
While my little sleeping baby
 Close in my arms is pressed;
And the feeling of awe and wonder
 I cannot understand,
That thrills and fills my being
 At the touch of my baby's hand.

'Tis mine to love and cherish,
 This little one in my care,
To keep her pure and sinless
 Shall be my constant prayer.
Wonderful love of the Father,
 Who for his children planned,
That we might know the sweetness
 Of the touch of a baby's hand.

Dear little hand! I love it!
 As I hold it in my own;
I feel its clasp on my heart strings,
 The strongest I have known.

Of the joys that come to mortals
This side of the better land,
The sweetest, the dearest, the purest
Is the touch of a baby's hand.

—Author unknown

169. A FATHER'S PRAYER

Give me a son, O Lord, who will be strong enough to know when he is weak, and brave enough to face himself when he is afraid—one who will be proud and unbending in honest defeat, and humble and gentle in victory.

Give me a son whose wishes will not take the place of deeds; a son who will know thee—and that to know himself is the foundation stone of true knowledge.

Lead him, I pray, not in the path of ease and comfort, but under the stress and strains of difficulties and challenges, let him learn to stand up in the storm. Let him also learn compassion for those who fail.

Give me a son whose heart will be clear, whose goal will be high —a son who will master himself before he seeks to master others—one who will reach into the future, yet never forget the past.

And after all these things, add enough of a sense of humor so he may always be serious, yet never take himself too seriously. Give him humility so he may always remember the simplicity of true wisdom and the meekness of true strength.

—*General Douglas McArthur*

170. THE CHALLENGE TO MODERN WOMAN

The challenge to woman today is the eternal challenge—that of being a godly woman.

The very phrase sounds strange in our ears. We never hear it today. We hear about every other kind of woman—smart women, career women, talented women, divorced women, sophisticated women; but so seldom do we hear of a godly woman—or of a godly man, either, for that matter.

I believe women come nearer fulfilling their God-given function in the home than anywhere else. It is a much nobler thing to be a good wife than to be Miss America. It is a greater achievement to establish a Christian home than it is to produce a second-rate novel, filled with filth. It is a far better thing in the realm of morals to be old-fashioned than to be ultra-modern. The world has enough women who have lost all their illusions and their faith.

The world has enough women who know how to be smart; it needs women who are willing to be simple.

The world has enough women who know how to be brilliant; it needs women who will be brave.

The world has enough women who are popular; it needs more who are pure.

—*Peter Marshall*

11
Faith and Courage

---

171. COURAGE OR FOOLISHNESS?

It takes a lot of courage
  To put things in God's hands,
To give ourselves completely—
  Our lives, our hopes, our plans—
To follow where he leads us
  And make his will our own—
But all it takes is foolishness
  To go the way alone!

—Author unknown

172. THINGS TO BELIEVE

Believe in yourself; you are God's creation.

Believe in your job; honest work is a form of worship.

Believe in this day; every minute contains an opportunity to serve God.

81

Believe in your family; create harmony and togetherness by working together.

Believe in your neighbor; friends are an important ingredient of a happy life.

Believe in the present; yesterday is gone and tomorrow may never come.

Believe in God's promise; he means it when he says, "I am with you always."

Believe in God's mercy; since God forgives you, you can forgive yourself and try again tomorrow.

173. WRITING YOUR STORY

No matter what else you are doing—
From cradle days through to the end—
You're writing your life's secret story;
Each day sees another page penned.

Each month ends a thirty-page chapter,
Each year means the end of a part,
And never an act is misstated,
Nor ever a wish from the heart.

Each day when you wake the book opens,
Revealing a page clean and white.
What thoughts and what words and what actions
Will cover its surface by night?

God leaves that to you—you're the writer,
And never one word shall grow dim
'Til some day you write the word "Finis,"
And give back your life book to him.

—Author unknown

5/25/86

174. LIFE IS A GIFT

Life is a splendid gift. There is nothing small in it. For the greatest grow by God's law from the smallest. But to live your life you must discipline it. You must not fritter it away. Make your thoughts, your words, your actions work toward the same end—not self but God and others.

—*Florence Nightingale*

175. FAITH

Lord, give me faith—to live from day to day,
With tranquil heart to do my simple part,
And, with my hand in thine, to go thy way.

Lord, give me faith—to trust, if not to know;
With quiet mind in all things thee to find,
And, child-like, go where thou wouldst have me go.

Lord, give me faith—to leave it all to thee,
The future is thy gift; I would not lift
The veil thy love has hung between it and me.

—John Oxenham

176. EVERYMAN'S CONFESSION

I confess, O Lord:

That often I let my mind wander down unclean and forbidden ways.

That often I deceive myself as to where my plain duty lies.

That often by concealing my real motives, I pretend to be better than I am.

That often my honesty is only a matter of policy.

That often my affection for my friends is only a refined form of caring for myself.

That often I do good deeds only that they may be seen of men, and shun evil ones only because I fear they may be found out.

O holy One, let the fire of thy love enter my heart to burn up all this meanness and hypocrisy. Make my heart as the heart of a little child.

—*John Baillie in* A Diary of Private Prayer

177. DEFINITIONS OF COURAGE

Courage is enduring
  For just one minute longer,
Courage is just holding on,
  Though others may be stronger.

Courage is a grappling hand
  When dreams we've had are fading,
Courage is just keeping on
  Enheartening and persuading.

Courage is a certain faith
  Expressed in act heroic,
Something deeper, deeper still
  Than simply being stoic.

Courage is a sensing
  Of our destiny, a tightening
Of the belt of circumstance,
  Though all its face be frightening.

Courage is a midnight song
  Through the deep darkness singing,
'Til the music born of faith
  Sets all life's rafters ringing.

Courage is a sensing
  That in spite of pain and sorrow,
God will see us through today
  And meet our needs tomorrow.

—Ruth Winant Wheeler

178. THE WEAVER

My life is but a weaving
  Between my Lord and me,
I cannot choose the colors
  He worketh steadily.

Ofttimes he weaveth sorrow,
  And I in foolish pride
Forget he sees the upper
  And I, the underside.

Not 'til the loom is silent
  And the shuttles cease to fly
Shall God unroll the canvas
  And explain the reason why.

The dark threads are as needful
  In the Weaver's skillful hand
As the threads of gold and silver
  In the pattern he has planned.

—Author unknown

12
Summer and
Leisure Time

179. SUPPORT YOUR CHURCH THIS SUMMER

The summer months are upon us. Many churches face the summer with fear and trembling. With more of our people going on vacations during the summer months, our attendance will obviously be lower than normal. But if those of us who are in town will be faithful to our Lord by supporting our church, our attendance will remain high. This will show others how much we love and support our church.

Ephesians 5:14-18 reminds us that time is precious. We need to use it wisely this summer. Here are some suggestions:

1. Be away as few Sundays as possible. Arrange your vacation to take the least time from the church and its activities.

2. If you're a teacher or leader, be sure that someone has consented to take over your responsibilities while you're gone.

3. Don't use the Lord's money for your vacation. There's no vacation from the responsibilities we have assumed as a church.

Let's make this summer one that glorifies the name of Jesus in all we do.

180. THE DANGER OF WEEKEND TRIPS

Isn't it wonderful when one lives close enough to relatives and friends to visit them over the weekend? What a joy it is to see our loved ones. It is convenient also to live near a lake or the ocean. But there is a great danger in these things, too. We can let weekend trips wreck our spiritual lives if we don't use this privilege sparingly. This is especially true during the summer months.

Don't let frequent weekend trips ruin your spiritual life and the ongoing ministry of your church.

181. SAVE THE SUMMER FOR THE SAVIOR

*Did you save your summer Sundays
For the Christ of Calvary?
Did you seek his holy presence,
Bowed in deep humility?*

*Have you led a lost and dying soul
To trust his saving grace?
Have you helped a broken spirit
Find his saving tenderness?*

*Did you heed his all-wise counsel?
Did you live for him each day?
When a task was set before you,
Did you always think to pray?*

*Did you witness for your Savior?
Claim the peace he offers you?
Have you done your best for Jesus?
He gave his life for you!*

—Inez Wyatt

182. DANGERS AND DISTRACTIONS OF SUMMER

We might as well face it: The dangers and distractions of summer seem to be here to stay. It is futile to ignore them, hoping they'll go away. Here are some of these ailments and liabilities that seem to bounce back every summer:

1. **Low temperature.** July, August, and September frequently bring an astonishing temperature inversion. As the physical thermometer goes up, the spiritual thermometer goes down.

2. **Overcrowding.** This problem happens mainly on Sundays and weekends — overcrowding on the golf courses, lakes, and highways. Overcrowding everywhere, except on church parking lots.

3. **Sleeping sickness.** The summer variety of this illness has nothing to do with the tsetse fly or tropical Africa. The symptoms include drowsiness and laziness. The brain and the backbone seem to be affected. This particular kind of sleeping sickness occurs mainly on Sunday mornings.

4. **The Sunday afternoon coma.** The hot summer weather seems to aggravate this condition. It keeps a person from attending the Sunday evening worship service.

5. **Midweek amnesia.** Warm weather apparently brings on a higher incidence of "Wednesday night forgetfulness." Church members can't remember the time, place, and purpose of the midweek prayer service.

These are some of the dangers and distractions that hit many Christians during the summer months. Be on the alert and try to avoid these problems in your home this year.

183. PARABLE OF THE VACATIONING CHRISTIANS

Now it came to pass as summer drew nigh that Mr. Church Member lifted up his eyes unto the hills and said:

"Lo, the hot days come and even now are at hand. Come, let us go unto the mountains, where cool breezes refresh us and glorious scenes greet our eyes."

"Thou speakest wisely," replied Mrs. Church Member. "Yet four things we must do before we go."

"Three things I can think of," responded Mr. Church Member.

"We must arrange for our flowers to be cared for, our pet to be fed, and our mail to be brought in, but the fourth eludes me."

"The fourth is like unto the first three, yet more important than all," Mrs. Church Member replied. "Thou shalt dig into thy purse and pay thy church tithes and offerings that the good name of the church shalt be preserved and that it may be well with thee. For verily I say unto thee, thou hast more money now than thou wilt when thou dost return."

And it came to pass that Mr. Church Member paid his tithe for the summer, and the church treasurer rejoiced greatly, saying, "Of a truth, there are those who care for the Lord's work." And it was so.

184. FOLLOWING GOD TO VBS

My dishes went unwashed today,
I didn't make the bed;
I took God's hand and followed him
To VBS instead.

Oh, yes, we went adventuring—
The children and I—
Exploring the whole Bible
For truths we can't deny,

My house was sure neglected,
I didn't sweep the stair—
In twenty years no one on earth
Will know, or even care.

But that I've helped a boy or girl
To noble adulthood grow,
In twenty years the whole wide world
May look, and see, and know.

—Author unknown

13
Finding and Following God's Will

185. HOW TO FIND GOD'S WILL

Here are some actions that can help you find God's will for your life:

Study your Bible regularly.

Pray to God frequently.

Worship God regularly.

Share your life struggles with one or two people.

Tithe your income through the church.

Look and listen for God in ordinary events of the day.

186. GOD WALKS WITH YOU

Though today you walk in sorrow,
You will not be alone—
There is one whose loving wisdom
Is far greater than your own.

Put your trusting hand in his
As a little child would do,
And he, like a loving Father,
Will guide and comfort you.

Day by day there will come to you
New faith, new hope, new light—
You'll find that stars unseen by day
Shine through the darkest night.

And though your heart is longing
For the dear one who's at rest,
You'll know, before the journey's end,
That God's dear ways are best!

—Jessie Home Fairweather

187. I MUST HAVE GOD!

I must have God!
I couldn't walk this thorny way
With stone beneath and cloud above,
Or meet the struggle of each day
Without his love.

I must have God!
I couldn't stand the hours at night
Or troubled day with all its length,
Or overlook what others say
Without his strength.

I must have God!
I couldn't carry on my lips
A song of cheer, a word to ease
The aching of another's heart
Without his peace.

I must have God!
I couldn't share the grief of those
Who need my help along life's way
Or comfort one in need of peace
Unless I pray.

—Amy Wellington

188. HOW TO FIND GOD'S WILL

How do you find God's will? Henry Drummond says the following eight actions are often helpful:

1. Pray.

2. Think.

3. Talk to wise people for their advice and counsel, but don't let them tell you exactly what you should do.

4. Beware of the bias of your own will, but don't be too afraid of it. God doesn't necessarily thwart a person's desire. Don't make the mistake of thinking that God's will and what you would like to do are always at odds.

5. Meanwhile, do the next logical thing that must be done. Doing God's will in small things is the best preparation for doing it in great things.

6. When the time of decision comes, act on the knowledge you have.

7. Never reconsider the decision, once you have acted on it.

8. Be patient. You may not find out until afterward, perhaps long afterward, that God was leading every step of the way.

189. QUESTIONS TO ASK BEFORE YOU DECIDE

Sometimes Christians have a hard time deciding what to do in a specific situation that calls for clear decision. Here are some questions to ask, based on specific passages from the Bible, that might help you in finding God's will:

1. Can you ask God to bless your decision? (Proverbs 10:22)

2. Can you thank God for it? (Colossians 3:17)

3. Are you doing this to the glory of God? (1 Corinthians 10:31)

4. Will your decision be a stumbling block to others? (1 Corinthians 8:9)

5. Are you doing this to please God rather than people? (Colossians 3:23)

92

6. Have you thought ahead about the consequences of your decision? (Galatians 6:7)

7. Would you want to be doing whatever you decide when Jesus returns? (Matthew 22:44)

8. Does it promote love? (Romans 13:8,10)

14
Inspiration
for Daily Living

190. TAKING LIFE SERIOUSLY

To realize how short life really is, think of a life span of seventy years as a single day—from 7:00 in the morning until 11:00 at night. If your age is:

15, the time is 10:25 a.m.

20, the time is 11:34 a.m.

25, the time is 12:42 p.m.

30, the time is 1:51 p.m.

35, the time is 3:00 p.m.

40, the time is 4:08 p.m.

45, the time is 5:16 p.m.

50, the time is 6:25 p.m.

55, the time is 7:34 p.m.

60, the time is 8:42 p.m.

65, the time is 9:51 p.m.

70, the time is 11:00 p.m.

This exercise reminds us that we don't have a lot of time to do the works of God. Let's get busy and make every day count for him.

191. SECRETS OF HAPPINESS

1. Keep skid chains on your tongue; always say less than you think.

2. Make promises sparingly, but keep your promises faithfully, no matter what it costs you.

3. Never let an opportunity pass to say a kind and encouraging word to someone. Praise good work, no matter who did it.

4. Show your interest in others. Let everyone you meet feel that you regard him as a person of importance.

5. Be cheerful. Keep the corners of your mouth turned up. Hide your pains, worries, and disappointments under a pleasant smile.

6. Keep an open mind on all issues. Discuss but don't argue. It is possible to disagree in a friendly way.

7. Let your virtues speak for themselves and refuse to talk about another person's vices. Discourage gossip. Make it a rule to say nothing unless it is something positive.

8. Be careful of other people's feelings.

9. Pay no attention to cutting or critical remarks about you; live so nobody will believe them.

10. Don't be too anxious about getting what you deserve. Do your work faithfully, and you will be respected and rewarded.

192. A PRAYER FOR THE DAY

Grant me, O Lord, the strength today
For every task which comes my way;
Cover my eyes and make me blind
To petty faults I should not find.

Open my eyes and let me see
The friend my neighbor tries to be;
Teach me, when duty seems severe,
To see my purpose shining clear.

Let me at noontime rest content,
The half-day bravely lived and spent;
And when the night slips down, let me
Unstained and undishonored be.

Grant me to live this one day through
Up to the best that I can do.

—Edgar A. Guest

193. HOW TO BE PERFECTLY MISERABLE

If your goal is to be miserable most of the time, the following ten actions will help you reach a state of misery in record time:

1. Think about yourself. Talk about yourself. Drop "I" as much as possible into every conversation.

2. Pay close attention to what people think and say about you.

3. Expect to be appreciated.

4. Cultivate suspicion, jealousy, and envy.

5. Be sensitive to slights. Never forgive a criticism.

6. Trust nobody but yourself.

7. Insist upon special consideration.

8. Demand that everyone agree with your views and opinions on everything.

9. Shirk your duties and responsibilities if you can.

10. Do as little as possible for other people.

194. TEN KEYS TO CREATIVE LIVING

1. Do something to solve your problems.

2. Accept and meet your obligations.

3. Adjust to the necessary.

4. Plan ahead with conservative optimism; set realistic goals.

5. Welcome new experiences; test new ideas.

6. Use your God-given talents.

7. Think, investigate, and decide for yourself.

8. Put your best into everything you do.

9. Share your joys and sorrows with others.

10. Reach out to help other people.

195. PRESCRIPTION FOR THE BLUES

If you wake in the morning and feel a bit blue,
And wonder whatever's the matter with you,
Don't go on a grouch the rest of the day
And make other people your penalty pay.

Just try to suppress it and put on a grin,
And no one will know what has happened within;
Just speak a kind word and do a good deed,
And others your action will certainly heed.

It was said long ago and today it's still true—
As you measure to others, it's given to you.

—Author unknown

196. JUST FOR TODAY

Just for today I will try to live through this day only and not tackle all my problems at once. I can do something for eight or ten hours that would depress me if I felt I had to keep it up for a lifetime.

Just for today I will be happy. Abraham Lincoln was right: "Most folks are as happy as they make up their minds to be."

Just for today I will try to strengthen my mind. I will study. I will learn something useful. I will not be a mental loafer. I will read something that requires effort, thought, and concentration.

Just for today I will adjust myself to what is and not try to adjust everything to my own desires. I will take things as they come and not protest against them.

Just for today I will exercise my soul in three ways: I will do something nice for someone; I will do something I don't want to do; and I will keep my feelings under control.

Just for today I will be agreeable. I will look as nice as I can, dress neatly, act courteously, and not try to improve anyone except myself.

Just for today I will set some goals. These will keep me from stumbling over two common problems: hurry and indecision.

Just for today I will have a quiet half hour all by myself. During this quiet time I will try to get a better perspective on my life.

Just for today "I will lift up mine eyes unto the hills, from whence cometh my help. My help cometh from the Lord, which made heaven and earth" (Psalm 121:1,2).

All these things I will do—just for today.

197. LOVE LIFE!

Artur Rubinstein, the famous pianist, was asked the secret of his success. Was it dedication, ability, discipline, hard work?

Mr. Rubinstein smiled. "It's hard to say, but one thing I do know: If you love life, life will love you back!"

What a wonderful insight! That philosophy explains how a man of eighty-three can continue to be so creative. Life is filled with exciting blessings for everybody. They're ours if we give enough of ourselves to life.

The giving starts when we get up in the morning. One person I know begins every day repeating some verses from the Bible. Then he talks more directly to God: "Lord, you've watched over me through the night. Now help me do something really great with this day."

Watch what happens to members of your family when you begin the day with a glow of good feeling and joy. They'll catch it, too. The same will hold true for the people you encounter all day long—in the office, at the restaurant, in the bus, in the elevator, at the grocery store.

Love life—and life will love you back.

—*Norman Vincent Peale*

15
Stewardship and Church Finance

198. THE MANY DIMENSIONS OF STEWARDSHIP

Christian stewardship means more than money and material possessions. Following are some other dimensions of life that we should give back to God:

1. **Time.** We are all rich here. You may be on a fixed income, but no one has more time than you. Every ministry takes time. Every prayer takes time. Every witness takes time. Every act of worship takes time. How much time will you commit to God?

2. **Talent and ability.** Look at all the things you can do! You have talents of all kinds. Some are big and some are small. Have you made them available to God? Can you be enthusiastic for Christ? The abilities you use daily are of great value where you work. Can the Lord use them? Don't wait for someone to ask before putting your talents to work for Christ.

3. **Creation.** God did a wonderful job in giving us our world. How are we taking care of it? This commitment means we should be careful not to litter or otherwise spoil God's beautiful world. It also means we should take care of the body that God

has given us; it's the temple of the Holy Spirit. Will you use wisely all that God has given you through his marvelous creation?

4. **Possessions.** This is more than money. It includes the tithe, but it also covers what we do with the nine-tenths that remains. The way we manage our resources is a part of Christian stewardship.

199. WORTHLESS RELIGION

Bulletin 9/6/85

A religion:

That does nothing,

That gives nothing,

That costs nothing,

That suffers nothing,

is worth nothing.

200. HOW TO OPERATE WITHOUT MONEY

We have discovered a way for our church to operate without money. Here's how it will work:

Each member will come to church during the week with a broom and a mop to keep his part of the building clean. Then a paid janitor won't be necessary.

Each member will take his turn playing the organ and directing the choir. No organist or choir director will be needed.

Each member will bring materials and tools to help maintain the building. Just think of the money we can save by doing it ourselves!

Each member must agree to spend at least a year as a missionary at his own expense on some foreign field. This will do away with the need for missions offerings.

Each member will go to college and seminary for the required years and fulfill all the qualifications to become a pastor. Then he will take his turn preaching, leading the services, conducting the funerals, performing marriages, calling on members and prospects, visiting the sick, and administering the business affairs of the church. This will save the expense of the pastor's salary.

If you don't like these ideas for operating the church, give ten percent of your income. Then the church can operate in the scriptural manner.

201. GOOD REASONS FOR TITHING

Tithing is a moral and spiritual obligation of the Christian for the following reasons:

1. **Law commands it.** The principle of tithing was known and practiced by ancient people. It was included in the Law of Moses and accepted by the prophets as one of the requirements of faith and duty (see Leviticus 27:30; Malachi 3:8).

2. **Stewardship includes it.** Faithful stewardship is required of the Christian. The stewardship of material possessions is expressed by the tithe. Jesus commended the tithe, and the apostle Paul approved the principle in his emphasis on regular and proportionate giving (see Matthew 23:23; 1 Corinthians 16:2).

3. **Needs demand it.** There is much physical and spiritual hunger in the world today. Millions of people are starving. Even more are without Christ and without hope. Are these conditions of no concern to us? World conditions should call forth our tithes and offerings (see Romans 1:14-15; 2 Corinthians 8:14).

4. **Love constrains it.** Tithing is not only an acknowledgement of debt; it is an expression of love and gratitude. The Christian has received much from God; therefore, he should give much back to him. It is a simple and easy matter to tithe when one recognizes God's love and mercy and gives himself and his money to the Lord (see 2 Corinthians 8:5; Luke 7:47).

5. **Results justify it.** The results of tithing are both material and spiritual. Tithing will provide adequately for all phases of the Lord's work: worship, missions, Christian education, and benevolence. Better still, it will deepen and enrich the spiritual life of the Christian and inspire faith, hope, and love in the hearts of others (see Luke 16:11; Malachi 3:10).

202. PORTRAIT OF A CHURCH BUDGET

Our church budget is more than dollars; it is also:

Missions, at home and around the world.

Ministry to persons in need.

Education of young and old alike in the ways of Christian discipleship.

Training in witnessing, Bible study, and missions.

Fellowship, as we work together as a church to proclaim the gospel in our own community and to the ends of the earth.

An opportunity for us to be personally involved in the exciting task of doing the work of Christ in the world today.

203. YOUR CHILD AND GIVING

Many parents ask, "Should my child turn in a pledge card?" or "Should my child have his own offering envelopes?"

Remember that children are imitators. They learn to do by doing. Their lifetime habits are formed in their early years. They give money more easily if it is in a special church envelope just like their parents have. Many two and three-year-olds start asking about their envelopes for church. Begin establishing giving patterns when there is natural interest like this on the part of your child.

If you want to complete a pledge card for your child, let him sign or print his own first name. You can write in his last name. The amount given is not as important as establishing the habit and letting your child participate in this part of the worship service. Talk with your child about how this money is used to tell others about Jesus.

204. WHAT IS MY TITHE?

My tithe is more than a check or a sum of money. It is:

My investment in a better community.

My aid to Christian youth.

My expression of faith in the future.

My gesture of good will.

My contribution to Christian education.

My outreach in healing and teaching through missions.

My vote for a Christian world.

My tithe is a holy offering, dedicated to God for the building of his kingdom on earth.

16
Patriotism
and Citizenship

205. MY COUNTRY, 'TIS OF THEE

My country, 'tis of thee,
Sweet land of liberty,
Of thee I sing.
Land where my fathers died,
Land of the pilgrims' pride,
From every mountain-side
Let freedom ring!

My native country, thee,
Land of the noble free,
Thy name I love.
I love thy rocks and rills,
Thy woods and templed hills;
My heart with rapture thrills
Like that above.

Let music swell the breeze,
And ring from all the trees
Sweet freedom's song.

Let mortal tongues awake,
Let all that breathe partake;
Let rocks their silence break,
  The sound prolong.

Our fathers' God, to thee,
Author of liberty,
  To thee we sing.
Long may our land be bright
With freedom's holy light;
Protect us by thy might,
  Great God, our King!

—Samuel F. Smith

206. A PRAYER FOR INDEPENDENCE DAY

God of our fathers, whose almighty hand has made and preserved our nation, grant that our people may understand what
it is they celebrate today.

May they remember how bitterly our freedom was won, the
down payment that was made for it, the installments that have
been made since the Republic was born, and the price that
must yet be paid for our liberty.

May we think of freedom not as the right to do as we please,
but as the opportunity to please to do what is right.

May it ever be understood that our liberty is under God and
can be found nowhere else.

May our faith be something that is not merely stamped upon
our coins, but expressed in our lives.

To the extent that America honors thee, wilt thou bless America. Keep her true as thou hast kept her free, and make her
good as thou hast made her rich.

—*Peter Marshall*

207. THIS IS MY NATIVE LAND

Breathes there the man with soul so dead
Who never to himself hath said,

"This is my own, my native land!"
Whose heart hath ne'er within him burned
As home his footsteps he hath turned
From wandering on a foreign strand?

If such there breathe, go, mark him well;
For him no minstrel raptures swell;
High though his titles, proud his name,
Boundless his wealth as wish can claim;
Despite these titles, power, and pelf,
The wretch, concentered all in self,
Living, shall forfeit fair renown,
And, doubly dying, shall go down
To the vile dust from whence he sprung,
Unwept, unhonoured, and unsung.

—Sir Walter Scott

208. LINCOLN'S GETTYSBURG ADDRESS

Fourscore and seven years ago our fathers brought forth on this continent a new nation, conceived in liberty and dedicated to the proposition that all men are created equal.

Now we are engaged in a great Civil War, testing whether that nation or any nation so conceived and so dedicated can long endure. We are met on a great battlefield of that war. We have come to dedicate a portion of that field as a final resting place for those who here gave their lives that that nation might live.

It is altogether fitting and proper that we should do this. But in a larger sense, we cannot dedicate, we cannot consecrate, we cannot hallow this ground. The brave men, living and dead, who struggled here have consecrated it far above our poor power to add or detract.

The world will little note nor long remember what we say here, but it can never forget what they did here. It is for us the living rather to be dedicated here to the unfinished work which they who fought here have thus far so nobly advanced. It is rather for us to be here dedicated to the great task remaining before us—

—That from these honored dead we take increased devotion to that cause for which they gave the last full measure of devotion.

—That we here highly resolve that these dead shall not have died in vain.

—That this nation under God shall have a new birth of freedom.

—And that government of the people, by the people, for the people, shall not perish from the earth.

17
Thanksgiving
Messages

209. THE SPIRIT OF THANKSGIVING

Insert Banquet
Braine
Nov 10, 1985

Father, we thank thee:
  For peace within our favored land,
  For plenty from thy bounteous hand,
  For means to give to those in need,
  For grace to help in thought and deed,
  For faith to walk, our hands in thine,
  For truth to know thy law divine,
  For strength to work with voice and pen,
  For love to serve our fellow men.
  For light the goal ahead to see,
  For life to use alone for thee—
Father, we thank thee.

—Author unknown

210. A PSALM OF THANKSGIVING

Hallelujah! I want to express publicly before his people my
heartfelt thanks to God for his mighty miracles. All who are

thankful should ponder them with me. For his miracles demonstrate his honor, majesty, and eternal goodness.

Who can forget the wonders he performs—deeds of mercy and of grace? He gives food to those who trust him; he never forgets his promises. He has shown his great power to his people by giving them the land of Israel, though it was the home of many nations living there. All he does is just and good, and all his laws are right, for they are formed from truth and goodness, and stand firm forever. He has paid a full ransom for his people; now they are always free to come to Jehovah (what a holy, awe-inspiring name that is).

How can men be wise? The only way to begin is by reverence for God. For growth in wisdom comes from obeying his laws. Praise his name forever (Psalm 111, The Living Bible).

211. FOR THESE I AM THANKFUL

There are so many things
To make life bright and gay,
That's why I sing a happy song
This glad Thanksgiving Day.

A baby's happy smile,
The handclasp of a friend,
A mother's love so true
Brings joys that never end.

The majesty of hills,
A tall and stately tree,
The wild and restless waves
Upon the mighty sea.

The fragrance of a rose,
The sun, the wind, the rain,
The silver stars, the moon,
A peaceful country lane.

The silence of the night,
The sparkling morning dew,
The music of the birds
That sing the whole day through.

For these and many more
I bring no price to pay—
Yet all these things are mine
This glad Thanksgiving Day.

—Helen L. Hazel

212. ALL THINGS BRIGHT AND BEAUTIFUL

All things bright and beautiful,
All creatures great and small,
All things wise and wonderful;
Our Father made them all.

Each little flower that opens,
Each little bird that sings;
He made their glowing colors,
He made their tiny wings.

Cold wind in the winter,
Pleasant summer sun,
Ripe fruits in the garden;
He made them every one.

He gave us eyes to see them,
And lips that we might tell
How good is God our Father
Who doeth all things well.

—Cecil F. Alexander

213. A THANKSGIVING PRAYER

We thank thee, God, for blessings—
The big ones and the small—
Thy tender love and mercy
That guards and keeps us all.

The fresh awakening of joy
That comes with morning light,
Sunlit hours to fill the day
And restful sleep at night.

The hope, the beauty, and the love
  That brighten each day's living—
We praise thee, and our hearts are filled
  With joy, and with thanksgiving.

The pride that's found in work well done,
  The love of those who care,
The peace of mind, the sweet content
  That comes with quiet prayer.

—Author unknown

18
Christmas
Messages

---

214. IN THE STABLE WHERE CHRIST WAS BORN . . .

Smell the stable. Smell the fresh cow dung. Smell the dampness of the cave, the water dripping along the side. Smell the donkeys and the cows. Smell the rancid straw, gleaming with animal saliva.

See the cobwebs, the hen with her little brood of chicks over in the corner, the crude and simple atmosphere of heaven's maternity ward.

Touch the warm backs of the animals as they chew their food in the stalls. Feel the manger, cushioned with new, clean straw.

Listen to the wind whistling through the gate. Listen again and you will hear the hundreds who still are up late at night, meandering through the streets of Bethlehem.

Notice the shaft of light that penetrates the gate as if it were focused from heaven upon this particular place. Look over in the far corner and you will see them. You will hear them. And you can touch them. The young mother with her newborn child. Her sturdy husband-to-be. The wondering shepherds.

How goes the stable of your life? Where is Christ being born in the shadows of your inner self? While the noises of life all around you continue, have you noticed what's happening inside your stable? Have you invited the wise to come and open their treasures to you? Have you allowed the lonely to come and celebrate the new things that are being born in your life? Are you listening to your dreams during the night?

—Hal Edwards, in "Faith at Work" *magazine, December 1978.*

215. O LITTLE TOWN OF BETHLEHEM

O little town of Bethlehem,
How still we see thee lie;
Above thy deep and dreamless sleep
The silent stars go by.

Yet in thy dark streets shineth
The everlasting light;
The hopes and fears of all the years
Are met in thee tonight.

O holy child of Bethlehem,
Descend to us, we pray;
Cast out our sin and enter in,
Be born in us today.

We hear the Christmas angels
The great glad tidings tell;
O come to us, abide with us—
Our Lord Emmanuel!

—Phillips Brooks

216. THE FRIENDLY BEASTS

Jesus our brother, strong and good,
Was humbly born in a stable rude,
And the friendly beasts around him stood,
Jesus our brother, strong and good.

"I," said the donkey, shaggy and brown,
"I carried his mother uphill and down,
I carried her safely to Bethlehem Town;

I," said the donkey, shaggy and brown.

"I," said the cow, all white and red,
"I gave him my manger for his bed,
I gave him my hay to pillow his head;
I," said the cow, all white and red.

"I," said the sheep with curly horn,
"I gave him my wool for his blanket warm,
He wore my coat on Christmas morn;
I," said the sheep with curly horn.

"I," said the dove, from the rafters high,
"Cooed him to sleep, my mate and I,
We cooed him to sleep, my mate and I;
I," said the dove, from the rafters high.

And every beast, by some good spell,
In the stable dark was glad to tell
Of the gift he gave Immanuel—
The gift he gave Immanuel.

—Twelfth-century Carol

217. EXCEPT YE BECOME AS CHILDREN

"Except ye become as children
Ye can no wise enter Heaven."
This is the voice of the Master
Speaking to us today
As we hear the children singing,
Lifting the ancient carols
In praise of the infant Jesus,
Born on a bed of hay.

Something there is that is holy
In the clear sweet voice of children;
Something there is of Jesus'
Own star in their lifted eyes,
And we who are worn and weary
Watching and harkening to them
Are suddenly lifted skyward,
So taken by surprise
That we once more are children,
Glad as they, and as wise.

—Grace Noll Crowell

19
The Bible and
Its Message

218. A FENCE OR A HOSPITAL?

One state passed a law forbidding the Bible to be read in the public schools, and the same state passed another law requiring that a Bible be placed in every prison cell in the state. What reasoning! A fence at the top of the cliff is much better than a hospital at the bottom.

219. THE BIBLE

Read then, but first thyself prepare
To read with zeal and mark with care;
And when thou readest what here is writ,
Let thy best practice second it:
So twice each precept read should be,
First in the Book and next in thee.

—Author unknown

220. GREAT PASSAGES OF THE BIBLE

221. TAKE THE REST BY FAITH

I am profitably engaged in reading the Bible. Take all of this book upon reason that you can and the balance by faith, and you will live and die a better man.

—Abraham Lincoln

222. THE ETERNAL WORD OF GOD

Generation follows generation, but the Bible lives on:

Nations rise and fall; yet it lives.

Kings and presidents come and go; yet it lives.

Doubted and criticized; yet it lives.

Condemned by unbelievers; yet it lives.

Misquoted and misinterpreted; still it lives.

The eternal Word of God will serve forever:

As a lamp to our feet.

As a light to our path.

As a gift of heaven.

As a standard for our lives.

As water for the thirsty.

As light for the unsaved.

As salvation for the sinner.

As grace for the Christian.

The eternal Word of God lives on. Make it a part of your life every day.

223. SOME GREAT PRAYERS OF THE NEW TESTAMENT

Prayers of Jesus:

The Lord's Prayer—Matthew 6:9-13.

Thanksgiving—Matthew 11:25,26.

For his followers—John 17.

In Gethsemane—Matthew 26:39.

For forgiveness of his enemies—Luke 23:34.

Prayer of the church in Jerusalem—Acts 4:24-30.

Stephen's prayer—Acts 7:60.

Paul's prayer for guidance—Acts 9:6.

224. THE BIBLE'S MESSAGE FOR SPECIAL TIMES

When things look hopeless, read Isaiah 40.

When tempted to do wrong, read Psalm 139.

If you are facing a crisis, read Psalm 46.

When you are discouraged, think about the words of Psalm 23.

If you are bored, read Psalm 103, or 104 and Job 38-40.

When business is bad, read Psalm 37.

When you are lonely, read Psalm 27.

When you are worried about loved ones, read Psalm 107.

When you plan your budget, read Luke 19.

To live successfully with others, follow the teachings of Romans 12.

If you are sick or in pain, read Psalm 91.

When you are traveling, carry the message of Psalm 121.

When you are tired, read Matthew 11:28-30 and Romans 8:31-39.

When everything seems to be going wrong, read 2 Timothy 3.

When friends reject you, hold fast to 1 Corinthians 13.

When you are placed in a position of great responsibility, read Joshua 1.

If you have experienced a severe loss, read Romans 8, especially the last paragraph.

20
Miscellaneous

---

225. THANK GOD FOR YOU

Thank God for you, good friend of mine,
Seldom is friendship such as thine;
How very much I wish to be
As helpful as you've been to me.
  Thank God for you.

When I recall from time to time
How you inspired this heart of mine,
I find myself inclined to pray,
"God bless my friend this very day."
  Thank God for you.

Of many prayer requests, one thou art
On whom I ask God to impart
Rich blessings from his storehouse rare,
And grant to you his gracious care.
  Thank God for you.

So often at the throne of grace,
There comes a picture of your face,

And then instinctively I pray
That God may guide you all the way.
Thank God for you.

Some day I hope with you to stand
Before the throne at God's right hand,
And say to you at journey's end,
You've been to me a faithful friend.
Thank God for you.

— Author unknown

226. A PASTOR'S JOB

The pastor teaches, but he must solicit his own classes. He heals, but he does it without pills, medicine, or scalpel. He is sometimes a lawyer, often a social worker, something of an editor, a bit of a philosopher and entertainer, a salesman, a decorative piece for public functions, and a student and scholar.

He visits the sick, marries people, buries the dead, comforts the sorrowing, admonishes sinners, and encourages the weary. He plans programs, appoints committees, and spends considerable time helping people with their difficulties. On top of all this, he prepares a sermon and preaches it on Sunday to faithful members of the congregation. Then on Monday he smiles when some person slaps him on the back and says, "One day a week. What a job!"

227. DIRECTIONS FOR CONGREGATIONAL SINGING

1. Sing with feeling and meaning. Don't sing as if you were half asleep. Lift up your voice with strength to show the power of the One whom you serve.

2. Don't sing so loudly, though, that you are heard above the rest of the congregation. Try to unite your voice with those of others in order to make one clear melodious sound.

3. Sing in time. Watch the music director, and follow his leading. Be especially careful not to sing too slowly. Sing as a happy, active, alert person sings who enjoys praising his God.

4. Above all, sing spiritually. Try to honor God in every word you sing. Aim at pleasing him more than yourself or any other person.

228. THE CALF PATH

One day through the primeval wood
A calf walked home, as good calves should,
But made a trail all bent askew—
A crooked path, as all calves do.

The trail was taken up next day
By a lone dog that passed that way;
And from that day, o'er hill and glade,
Through those old woods a path was made.

And many men wound in and out,
And dodged and turned and bent about,
And uttered words of righteous wrath
Because 'twas such a crooked path.

This crooked lane became a road,
Where many a poor horse with his load
Toiled on beneath the burning sun,
And traveled some three miles in one.

The years passed on in swiftness fleet,
The road became a village street;
And thus, before men were aware,
A city's crowded thoroughfare.

Each year a hundred thousand rout
Followed this zigzag calf about,
And o'er his crooked journey went
The traffic of a continent.

They followed still his crooked way
And lost one hundred years a day;
For thus such reverence is lent
To well-established precedent.

For men are prone to go it blind
Along the calf-path of the mind,
And work away from sun to sun
To do what other men have done.

They follow in the beaten track,
And out and in, and forth and back,
And still their devious course pursue,
To keep the path that others do.

They keep the path a sacred groove
Along which all their lives they move;
But how the wise old wood-gods laugh
Who saw the first primeval calf.

—Sam Walter Foss

229. NONE INDISPENSABLE

Sometimes when you're feeling important,
Sometimes when your ego's in bloom,
Sometimes when you take it for granted
You're the best qualified in the room.

Sometimes when you feel that your going
Would leave an unfillable hole,
Just follow this simple instruction
And see how it humbles your soul:

Take a bucket and fill it with water,
Put your hand in it up to the wrist;
Pull it out and the hole that's remaining
Is the measure of how you'll be missed.

You may splash all you please as you enter—
You can stir up the water galore—
But stop and you'll find in a minute
That it looks quite the same as before.

The moral in this example
Is do just the best you can;
Be proud of yourself, but remember—
There is no indispensable man.

—Author unknown

230. MID-YEAR RESOLUTIONS REVIEW

You've probably forgotten the resolutions you made at the beginning of this year. Here are a few you might consider as a mid-year resolutions review. They're guaranteed to make you a better person, no matter when you observe them:

Keep me from the habit of thinking I must say something on every subject on every occasion.

Release me of the burden of trying to straighten out everybody's affairs.

Make me thoughtful but not moody; helpful but not bossy.

Keep my mind free of the recital of endless details. Give me wings to get to the point.

Seal my lips on my aches and pains. They are increasing, and my love of hearing them is becoming sweeter as the years go by.

I ask not for improved memory but a growing humility when my memory seems to clash with the memory of others.

Teach me the glorious lesson that, occasionally, I may be mistaken.

Give me the ability to see good things in unexpected places and talents in unexpected people.

Record
of Publication

Item No.	Where Published	When Published
11	Bulletin	1/6/85
149	"	1/13/85
168	Bulletin	1/20/85
19	Bulletin	5/19/85
106	Bulletin	5/19/85
171	"	6/2/85
2	Bulletin	6/9/85
160	Bulletin	6/16/85

Item No.	Where Published	When Published
————	—————————	————
————	—————————	————
————	—————————	————
————	—————————	————
————	—————————	————
————	—————————	————
————	—————————	————
————	—————————	————
————	—————————	————
————	—————————	————
————	—————————	————
————	—————————	————
————	—————————	————
————	—————————	————
————	—————————	————
————	—————————	————
————	—————————	————
————	—————————	————
————	—————————	————
————	—————————	————

Item No.	Where Published	When Published
_____	_____	_____
_____	_____	_____
_____	_____	_____
_____	_____	_____
_____	_____	_____
_____	_____	_____
_____	_____	_____
_____	_____	_____
_____	_____	_____
_____	_____	_____
_____	_____	_____
_____	_____	_____
_____	_____	_____
_____	_____	_____
_____	_____	_____
_____	_____	_____
_____	_____	_____
_____	_____	_____
_____	_____	_____
_____	_____	_____

Item No.	Where Published	When Published